D1261490

CAFÉ DEGAS

COOKBOOK

CAFÉ DEGAS
COOKBOOK

Troy Gilbert with Jerry Edgar
and Jacques Soulas

Photography by Sara Essex Bradley
and Jerry Edgar

Art by Jacques Soulas

Foreword by Robert D. Peyton

PELICAN PUBLISHING COMPANY
GRETNA 2011

Library of Congress Cataloging-in-Publication Data

Gilbert, Troy A.
  Café Degas cookbook / Troy Gilbert with Jerry Edgar and Jacques
Soulas ; photography by Sara Essex Bradley and Jerry Edgar ; art
by Jacques Soulas ; foreword by Robert D. Peyton.
     p. cm.
  Includes index.
  ISBN 978-1-58980-766-2 (alk. paper)
  1. Cooking, French. 2. Cooking—Louisiana—New Orleans. 3. Café
Degas (New Orleans, La.) I. Edgar, Jerry. II. Soulas, Jacques. III.
Title.

  TX719.G595 2011
  641.59763'35—dc22

                                            2010030683

Printed in Singapore

Published by Pelican Publishing Company, Inc.
1000 Burmaster Street, Gretna, Louisiana 70053

SOMMAIRE

AVANT-PROPOS

Picture a spring day in New Orleans. You're walking along Esplanade Avenue, near the Fairgrounds, City Park, and the New Orleans Museum of Art. You've made reservations at a restaurant called Café Degas, and it will be your first time dining there.

As you walk under the live oaks that shade either side of Esplanade, you approach a small cottage with a covered deck that faces the street. You walk up a short pathway through their lush garden to the narrow doors and enter. Just to your left is a small bar, and you're early, so you sit down for a predinner drink. You notice that everyone in the place seems to know each other—or at least that's the way it appears. Pretty soon, you're having a conversation with the person next to you, whether you're the gregarious sort or not.

When it's time to be seated and you are heading to the dining room, you see a tiny window into a kitchen that seems too small to be useful. As you are led to your table, you realize the dining room is a roofed porch open on three sides. You can see heavy plastic drapes that would be employed during inclement weather, but because it's nice, the restaurant is open to the elements, allowing you to enjoy the warm evening air.

You are seated in a comfortable, casual chair, and your server greets you with familiarity, as though you've been here before. The dining room is small, but there is enough space between tables that you don't feel cramped. To the contrary, from the moment you entered Café Degas, you felt comfortable.

You take a look at the menu while you nibble on a baguette spread with butter. The restaurant takes its French heritage seriously. Classic bistro fare predominates, but there's also a small page of daily specials that break from the French mold. You order, and when the food arrives, you realize that despite its size, the kitchen produces some serious food, with flavors that seem too big to have come from such a small space.

Maybe you started with the onion soup, a classic version topped with gratinéed cheese. Perhaps you preferred the escargots in butter, garlic, and Pernod, or you went with the mussels steamed in white wine with fennel. If you were in the mood for meat, you may have chosen the hanger steak as your entrée or the Dijon-crusted rack of lamb. If you were looking for something lighter, you could have gone with the niçoise salad made with yellowfin tuna.

Or it's possible you decided to choose one of the ever-changing specials. This night they include a truffled chive vichyssoise; a fennel-pollen-roasted yellow edge grouper served with le Puy lentils; and a pan-roasted loin of baby Texas antelope with a cumin-scented black bean cake, jicama slaw, and an ancho-chile demi-glace.

Desserts are described on a board, and if you aren't seated adjacent to it, your server brings it over for you to peruse. Like the rest of the menu, the desserts are excellent, a mix of the down-home and the ambitious. Can you remember the last time you saw floating islands on a menu? You have a coffee to wrap things up and decide you'll be returning to Café Degas.

You've just had the experience that a great many New Orleanians and visitors to the city have had since 1986. It's the experience I had, and I've been a frequent guest at the restaurant ever since.

The offerings at Café Degas have been centered on the food of Parisian bistros since it opened, and that's still the mainstay of the menu. Between 2004 and 2010, however, chef Ryan Hughes both strengthened that part of the menu and used the freedom owners Jerry Edgar and Jacques Soulas gave him to stretch expectations with his specials. Soulas explains the philosophy behind the menu by saying that there is always a desire for staying power, for not giving up on the classics, but at the same time, he understands the restaurant has to offer the opportunity for creativity.

Hughes was serious about the French side of the menu. Before he entered the kitchen, for example, the mussels were cooked with white wine, garlic, herbs, and butter, a perfectly respectable take on the dish. He switched the preparation slightly, to seafood stock, fresh fennel, orange juice, and Herbsaint—still unmistakably French but with a bit of personal creativity. Hughes was behind a move to install a fryer in the kitchen in order to properly cook frites, and he instituted a much more ambitious cheese program. He worked to source ingredients from local producers but also searched far afield for such products as the boudin noir that the restaurant imports from California.

Now, Chef Laurent Rochereux fine-tunes and further advances the culinary helm at Café Degas. To Rochereux, a bistro-style restaurant should always offer certain standard dishes, it should be a neighborhood restaurant, and the prices should be reasonable. It's perhaps counterintuitive, but Rochereux believes that the more casual feel of the restaurant gives him even more freedom to explore exotic ingredients in his specials. In a fancier restaurant, diners might be too intimidated to try a special of antelope but because of the trust regular diners have developed in the restaurant, when the chef offers it, they eat it up.

As a native of France, Rochereux is an ideal fit at Café Degas. He loves to surprise diners who come in for the first time, see the casual atmosphere of the restaurant, and are blown away by his specials. Simply put, he loves coming to work every day. That's a feeling that is evident throughout the staff at Café Degas, and it's infectious. It's part of why the restaurant is so welcoming and why so many of its patrons come back time and again.

Robert D. Peyton

PRÉFACE

A bit over ten years ago and with the slight trepidation of one headed to a restaurant to dine alone, I made the quick trek across City Park to Café Degas. It was a cooling fall evening and I was looking for a restaurant where I knew I could sit at the bar and enjoy an early dinner and a glass of wine before heading out Uptown. It was not my first venture to the restaurant, but it was one of my more enlightening, and it started for me a real love for the place and the people.

It was still light outside and the little French doors leading from the garden balcony were open. Inside, the bar is intimate, if not small, with five bar stools that focus your attention on the bustle of the bar, the maître d', wait staff, and the entering and exiting patrons. If the kitchen is the heart of Café Degas, then the bar is its soul.

I sat in the corner—which to this day is still my normal place—and immediately became engrossed in the characters and conversations. Seated to my right were two guys who either worked at the fairgrounds or spent a majority of their time at the nearby track, pre-hipster smoky brown fedoras and old New Orleans' channel accents in tow. To the right was a pair of Europeans who, between their wine, French bread, and escargots, spoke a mix of French and English with a tenor that conveyed their ease of place. Throughout, the wait staff navigated their way and made their rounds to the sidebar for their drink and food orders and with them a quick cadence of jovial bickering and interplay followed.

What I learned unencumbered by distractions that night is that the wait staff, bartender, back-of-house staff, and maître d' are all there for your dining pleasure. But more so, they are the recurring, primary actors in a freestyle play that is staged every night at Café Degas. As quiet as I was and engrossed in my eavesdropping, I did not remain in the audience for long. I was rapidly incorporated by the crew and patrons and I stayed for the evening until close.

With ten years under my belt as a regular at the restaurant and especially now having worked with the owners and chefs in putting together this book, I too have an ease and sense of place at Café Degas. I, like so many others, recognize it as part of the central nervous system of Faubourg St. John, whose relaxed and European feel draws in patrons from throughout the city.

The restaurant is like a beloved aunt who calls you into her kitchen as a kid to talk and laugh while she cooks or like a slightly defrocked European society lady whom you wish would invite you to dinner more often. The restaurant is home to many a young couple's nervous and successful first date and has the feel of a confident lover wooed by men and women alike.

Café Degas has held the beat of the French presence in New Orleans since 1986, and it is comforting to find it normal to watch individuals wearing berets play pétanque in the green and art-filled park across Esplanade. While most restaurants are incredibly generous with their cuisine, the owners of Café Degas can always be counted on to join in and feed the multitudes who support altruistic events in the city. The restaurant is a continuing host of one of the city's great Bastille Day celebrations, including a regatta on Lake Pontchartrain, and for many years they, along with others, hosted the colorful Degas' Days Festival on Bayou St. John, replete with nineteenth-century costuming and collegiate sculling regattas, a further expression of their love and understanding of New Orleans.

When Jerry Edgar, Eddie Kurtz, Jacques Soulas, and Bridgitte Fredy came together from varied walks of life to create what is now an icon of Faubourg St. John and New Orleans dining, none would have guessed what a strong run would follow. In fact, I truly think they are only now hitting their stride. Having taken the name from Edgar Degas, the famed French Impressionist who resided in New Orleans just down the street on Esplanade from 1872 to 1873, they helped reinvigorate the classic French roots of a town that was coming back into its own after languishing for a pair of decades. And they did this in the way the city respects more than anything—through food, community, and ambiance.

Photograph by Fridgeir Helgason

In a great, almost literary twist of fate, one of the restaurant's first employees was David Musson, who bears an uncanny likeness to the painter Degas. This is no coincidence as he is a descendent of the painter's family, specifically of Estelle Musson, whose portrait is one of the more famous of Degas' works and resides in the New Orleans Museum of Art a short few blocks away. David is still with the restaurant and it is always a great pleasure to catch a moment with him as he sips on a glass of cabernet while waiting on an order.

CAFÉ DEGAS COOKBOOK

Over the years, the kitchen staff and chefs who have presided over that famously small kitchen have produced what has become for many a New Orleanian their favorite weekly meal. During my tenure as a regular, the pleasantly vexing issues have come from straying from my stalwart favorite dishes to enjoy Chef Ryan Hughes' and now Chef Laurent Rochereux's special daily menu choices. In all my years of fine dining, I have never had another chef personally take down my number and call me when a special that I love reappears on the menu some four or five months later—an amazing feat from an individual whose time is so valuable.

In a way it is bothersome to me that in preparing this book, I learned how to reproduce many of the tastes and flavors of Café Degas in my home kitchen, because a book can only convey but an impression of the full Degas experience. Luckily, I, like all New Orleanians, have the luxury to now open this book, tilt my head with a wry smile, and then close it, knowing that the restaurant, her energy, and her people are just there now, down on Esplanade Avenue.

Troy Gilbert

REMERCIEMENTS

It is nearly impossible to individually name and thank all the countless souls and patrons who since 1986 have made this restaurant a success and, in many respects, a true family. Yet, there are a few individuals whom we must thank personally. Denmon Britt, our first chef at Café Degas, really helped us create the restaurant's identity. David Musson has been with us since day one and is coincidentally related to Edgar Degas. Our current chef, Laurent Rochereux, and our past chef of six years, Ryan Hughes, have elevated all of the creations coming from our small kitchen. Jim and Jan Jeter have been found at least once a week dining at our restaurant since we opened and have become great friends of ours. Most importantly, to single out the one individual to whom we could dedicate this book, it would hands down be Jacqueline Guiot. She is the true soul of Café Degas.

Through the years, the incredible dedication of our staff, chefs, and loyal customers has helped us weather hardships, but more importantly, they have joined us in celebrating the better times. All of these experiences have come together and truly defined our lives. We are forever grateful.

Jerry Edgar &
Jacques Soulas

It is no surprise that over all the years I have frequented Café Degas (and somewhere along the line getting officially designated as a "regular"), I've gotten to know the owners, much of the staff, and my other regular cohorts. It is these people who make this restaurant a true French and New Orleans neighborhood refuge filled with characters and life in a city overflowing with these influences. I do not exaggerate when I say that I love this restaurant and hold dear my many experiences there.

I was absolutely thrilled to put together this book. The restaurant deserves to have a cookbook that will capture its personality and flavor in every aspect. I cannot give thanks enough to all who participated in this process, encouraged me, and made it a truly fun endeavor, as well as to Pelican and all involved for seeing the wisdom in publishing this book.

Specifically I can only express my sincerest gratitude to Jerry and Jacques for opening up their world behind the scenes to me and for their art and photographic contributions, which add a lasting, personal touch to this book; Chef Ryan, Chef Laurent, and Chef Denmon Britt for their great expertise and assistance in capturing the flavors and culinary vision of Café Degas; Robert Peyton for writing the foreword—he really needed no coaxing as he loves the restaurant; and Sara Essex Bradley for her photos, which superbly capture the creative energy and ambiance of Café Degas. Last, but not least, I have to thank the staff and Degas' truly patient bartender, Nick Varisco, not only for his drink recipes but also for putting up with me.

Cheers and I hope to see all of you at Degas' in short order. How about next Friday?

Troy Gilbert

CAFÉ DEGAS

COOKBOOK

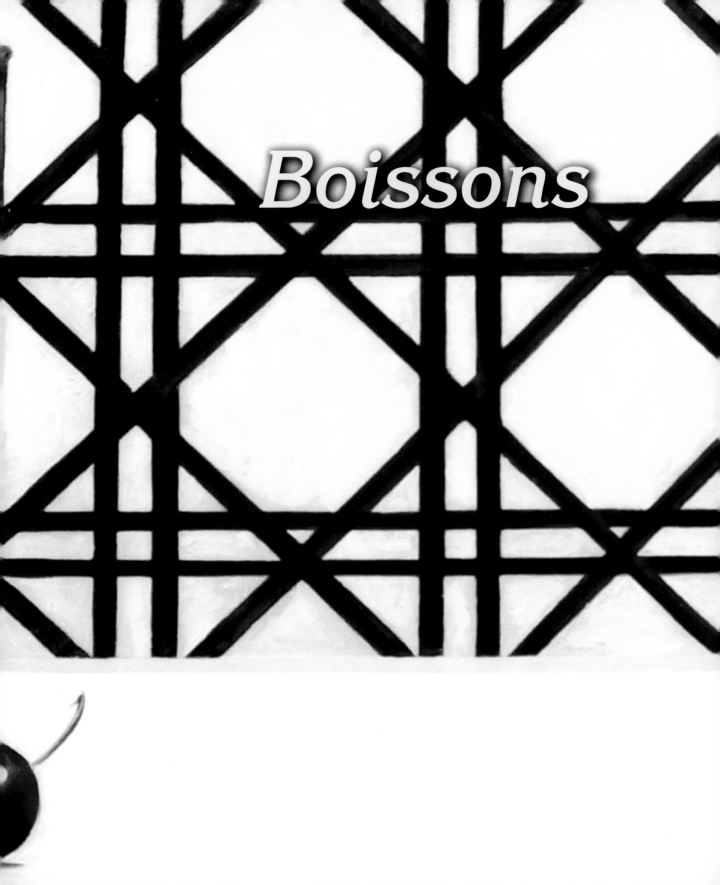

Boissons

THE UNCLE NICK
Serves 1

2 oz. espresso
2 oz. Baileys Irish cream
1 oz. Godiva Milk Chocolate Liqueur

Méthode:
Pour espresso over ice into a water glass. Add Irish cream and chocolate liqueur. Stir gently and serve.

CHOCOLATE MARTINI
Serves 1

Club soda
2 oz. Grey Goose vodka
2 oz. Godiva Milk Chocolate
    Liqueur

1 oz. Baileys Irish cream
Hershey's Chocolate Syrup

Méthode:
Fill a martini glass with ice and club soda to chill. In a cocktail shaker, combine vodka, chocolate liqueur, and Irish cream. Shake well. Empty martini glass and garnish with Hershey's Chocolate Syrup to taste. Strain contents of shaker into glass and serve.

FRENCH MARTINI
Serves 1

Club soda

2 oz. Grey Goose vodka

½ oz. Chambord

2½ oz. pineapple juice

1 maraschino cherry

Méthode:

Fill a martini glass with ice and club soda to chill. In a cocktail shaker with ice, combine vodka, Chambord, and pineapple juice. Shake well, strain into empty martini glass, garnish with maraschino cherry, and serve.

MOJITO
Serves 1

15-20 fresh mint leaves

4 oz. Mount Gay Eclipse Rum
   or Sailor Jerry Spiced Rum

Juice of ½ lime

¾ oz. simple syrup

Club soda

Méthode:

Place mint leaves into a cocktail shaker, add ice, and muddle gently. Add rum, lime juice, and simple syrup. Shake well. Strain over ice into a water glass, filling to within 1½ inches of rim. Top with club soda, garnish with mint leaves, and serve.

PIMM'S CUP
Serves 1

8-10 slices English cucumber
4 oz. Pimm's No. 1
Ginger ale

Méthode:
Place cucumber in a cocktail shaker and muddle well. Add Pimm's and ice to shaker and shake well. Fill water glass with ice then strain contents of shaker into glass, filling to within 1½ inches of rim. Top with ginger ale. Garnish with cucumber slice and serve.

BELLINI
Serves 1

1½ oz. Mathilde peach liqueur
4-5 oz. Champagne, chilled
Grenadine

Méthode:
Into a Champagne flute, pour Mathilde peach liqueur. Fill flute with Champagne. Add 1 drop grenadine for color. Stir and serve.

STREETCAR
Serves 1

Club soda
2 oz. Citadelle gin
2½ oz. Mathilde pear liqueur

Juice of ½ lemon
1 pear slice

Méthode:
Fill a martini glass with ice and club soda to chill; set aside. In a cocktail shaker, combine gin, pear liqueur, and lemon juice. Shake well. Empty martini glass and garnish with pear slice. Strain contents of shaker into glass. Serve.

FRENCH 75
Serves 1

1½ oz. Pierre Ferrand Grande Champagne cognac
4-5 oz. Champagne, chilled

Méthode:
Into a Champagne flute, pour cognac. Fill with Champagne and serve.

ST. GERMAIN COCKTAIL
Serves 1

½ oz. St. Germain Liqueur
5-6 oz. Champagne, chilled
Club soda

Méthode:
Pour St. Germain Liqueur into a Champagne flute. Add Champagne, filling flute to within ½ inch of rim. Top with a splash of club soda and serve.

SAZERAC
Serves 1

⅛ oz. Herbsaint   ¼ oz. simple syrup
4 dashes Angostura bitters   1½ oz. rye whiskey
8 dashes Peychaud's bitters

Méthode:
Pour Herbsaint into a rocks glass; set aside. In a cocktail shaker, combine bitters then add simple syrup. Pour in whiskey. Add ice and gently stir; do not shake. Discard Herbsaint and add three ice cubes and a lemon twist to emptied rocks glass. Strain mixture over ice and serve.

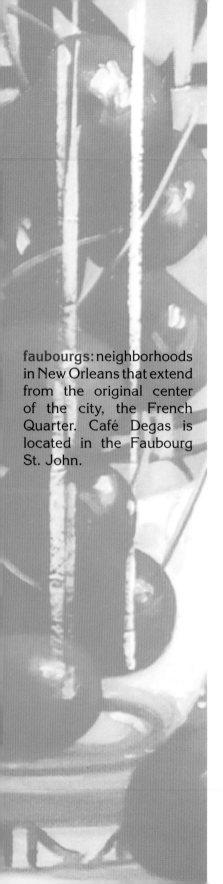

DEGAS' ABSINTHE 61
Serves 1

1 oz. Nouvelle Orléans
    Absinthe Supérieure
4-5 oz. Champagne

Méthode:
Chill absinthe in a shaker with ice. Strain into a Champagne flute and top with chilled Champagne. Serve.

faubourgs: neighborhoods in New Orleans that extend from the original center of the city, the French Quarter. Café Degas is located in the Faubourg St. John.

THE FAUBOURG ST. JOHN
Serves 1

1 oz. Nouvelle Orléans
    Absinthe Supérieure

3 oz. lemon juice
½ tbsp. sugar

Méthode:
Mix absinthe, lemon juice, and sugar together into a highball glass over ice. Stir well.

ABSINTHE CREPEAU
Serves 1

1½ oz. Maker's Mark bourbon   1½ oz. Cointreau
1½ oz. Nouvelle Orléans   Juice of ½ lime
     Absinthe Supérieure

Méthode:
Fill a martini glass with ice and club soda to chill. In a cocktail shaker with ice, combine bourbon, absinthe, Cointreau, and lime juice. Shake well. Empty martini glass and strain contents of shaker into glass. Serve.

TRADITIONAL ABSINTHE
Serves 1

3 oz. Nouvelle Orléans   5 oz. ice-cold water
     Absinthe Supérieure   1 sugar cube

Méthode:
Rest a perforated spoon across the rim of a heavy absinthe glass so that any liquid poured through the spoon's bowl will enter the glass. Place a single cube of sugar on top of the spoon. Slowly pour absinthe over the sugar cube and into the glass. Using caution, light the sugar cube on fire with a match. Allow the sugar cube to burn for a couple of seconds before dripping ice-cold water from a glass carafe onto the cube and into the glass. The sugar cube will slowly dissolve and drip down into the absinthe below. Continue dripping the water until you have reached a mixture of about 5:3 or filled the glass. Stir in the remains of the sugar cube. Enjoy—in moderation—and say hi to the Green Fairy.

SPICED MULLED WINE
Serves 12-14

4 cups sugar
4 cups orange juice
6 cinnamon sticks
15 cloves, whole
4 star anise seeds
20 pink peppercorns

6 orange slices, plus zest
1 cup simple syrup
1 cup Myers's Original Dark
  Rum
2 bottles red wine

Méthode:
In a large saucepot, boil first seven ingredients together for five minutes. Allow to cool and strain if desired. Combine simple syrup, rum, and wine in saucepot; bring to a light simmer. Do not allow to boil. Serve hot.

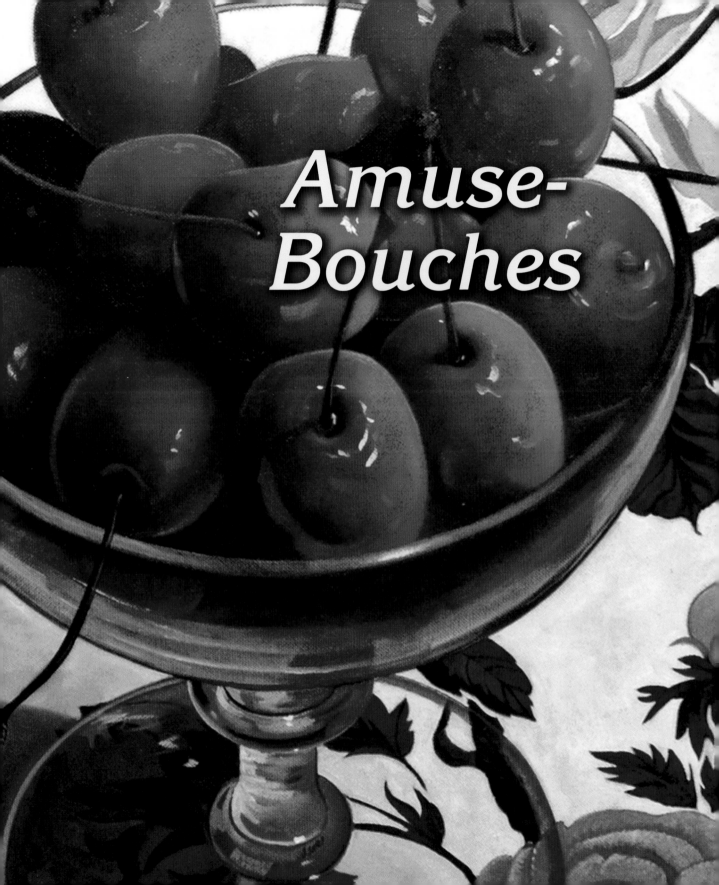

Amuse-Bouches

ESCARGOTS *with* HERBSAINT
Serves 10-12

1 can snails (72 count),
   good quality
2 tbsp. butter
1 tbsp. salt
1 tsp. pepper
2 tbsp. chopped parsley

2 tsp. minced garlic
1 tsp. diced shallots
2 tbsp. Herbsaint or other
   anise-flavored liqueur
6 tbsp. red wine
Escargot Butter

Méthode:
Drain and rinse snails well. Dry very well. Sauté snails in a large pan in butter with salt and pepper. Add parsley, garlic, and shallots and continue to sauté until well combined. Remove from pan and set aside. Deglaze pan with liqueur. Add red wine and reduce by half. Pour red wine reduction over snails. Allow to cool then portion into escargot dishes, 7 per person. Top with Escargot Butter and broil for 5 minutes.

ESCARGOT BUTTER

1 cup butter
5 tbsp. minced shallots
3 tbsp. minced garlic
1 cup chopped parsley
3 tbsp. thyme
3 tsp. Worcestershire sauce

1 tsp. Tabasco or Crystal hot
   sauce
4 tbsp. Herbsaint
2 tbsp. salt
2 tbsp. black pepper
2 tbsp. lemon juice

Méthode:
Melt the butter and then combine all ingredients in a food processor; mix until smooth. Serve over escargots.

quatre épices: pepper, cloves, nutmeg, and ginger

BOUDIN NOIR
Makes about 5 lb.

Hog casings (found at specialty butchers)
5 onions, finely diced
2 tbsp. chopped garlic
3 oz. lard or duck fat, divided
4 green apples, peeled and quartered
¼ cup Calvados
1½ lb. fatback
2 lb. pork shoulder
1 bunch flat-leaf parsley, finely chopped
5 tbsp. kosher salt
2 tbsp. black pepper
2 tsp. nutmeg
1½ tsp. *quatre épices*
2 cups whole milk
10 cups fresh pig's blood

Méthode:
Soak casings in warm water for 15 minutes. Rinse and set aside in cold water. In a pan with a lid, sweat onions and garlic in lard over low heat until translucent, reserving 2 tbsp. lard for the apples, then allow to cool to room temperature. Sear apples until brown in reserved lard, deglaze pan with Calvados, and chill. Grind fatback and pork with a fine blade. Combine all ingredients, except the blood and casings, in the bowl of a stand mixer with a paddle attachment. Mix on low, slowly adding the blood. Stuff casings and poach in 185-degree salted water for about 18 minutes or until internal temperature reaches 165 degrees. Remove and rinse with cold water. Serve on a bed of choucroute (recipes follow).

rondeau: a shallow, wide, straight-sided pot with loop handles

PEAR *and* BRANDY CHOUCROUTE
Serves 6-8

2 tbsp. butter, divided	Salt and pepper to taste
1 tsp. ground caraway, divided	1 oz. honey
1 tsp. ground fennel, divided	1 oz. sugar
1 tsp. ground mustard seed, divided	½ cup cane vinegar
	2 pears, sliced
1 head green cabbage, sliced	1 cup brandy

Méthode:

In a rondeau pan, melt 1 tbsp. butter with ½ tsp. caraway, ½ tsp. fennel, and ½ tsp mustard seed. Add cabbage and sauté until al dente. Season with salt and pepper to taste and add honey, sugar, and cane vinegar. Reduce by half over medium heat. Remove from heat and cool on a sheet pan. In the same rondeau pan, melt the rest of the butter and sauté pears, stirring gently until they are lightly browned. Season with remaining spices and deglaze with brandy. Allow to cool, then fold into cabbage mixture.

APPLE CHOUCROUTE
Serves 4-5

¼ cup bacon or duck fat
½ cup butter, divided
1½ heads green cabbage, sliced
½ head red cabbage, sliced
3 onions, julienned
1 tbsp. chopped garlic
Salt and pepper to taste
¼ cup honey
1 tbsp. sugar
½ cup cane vinegar
4 green apples, peeled and quartered
½ tsp. ground caraway
½ tsp. ground fennel,
½ tsp. mustard seed
½ cup white wine
¼ cup vodka

Méthode:
Melt ¼ cup butter in a rondeau. Render the bacon or duck fat in the pan with the butter. Add the cabbages, onions, and garlic; sauté until al dente. Season with salt and pepper, honey, sugar, and vinegar. Over low heat reduce by half. Remove to a sheet pan and allow to cool. In the rondeau, melt the remainder of the butter and sauté apples until lightly browned. Season with caraway, fennel, and mustard seed, then deglaze with wine and vodka. Reduce by one-third over low heat. Remove from heat and cool. Once cool, fold into cabbage mixture. Serve.

Note:
Choucroutes are delicious when served as a bed for fatty sausages such as andouille, pork, and lamb. A more traditional Alsatian choucroute would add juniper berries and gin instead of vodka and would call for boiled and peeled potatoes.

FROG LEGS PROVENÇALE
Serves 4-6

9 pairs frog legs, cleaned
Kosher salt to taste
Ground black pepper to taste
½ cup breadcrumbs
¼ cup Panko
1 tbsp. grated Parmesan
   cheese

2 tsp. chopped fresh parsley
1 cup all-purpose flour
2 eggs
¼ cup olive oil
2 tbsp. whole butter

Méthode:
Remove saddle from each pair of frog legs and discard. Season legs with salt and pepper. In one bowl, combine breadcrumbs and Panko with Parmesan, parsley, and salt and pepper. Pour flour into a separate bowl. In a third bowl, beat eggs. Dredge legs in flour then wash in the eggs. Dredge legs in the breadcrumb mixture twice to ensure they are thickly coated. Set legs aside. Heat oil and butter in a large sauté pan until just below the smoking point. Pan-fry legs until brown on all sides (about 4 minutes). Drain on paper towels. Drizzle with Sauce Provençale and serve.

SAUCE PROVENÇALE

½ bunch watercress
1 cup white wine
1 tbsp. chopped garlic
1 tbsp. lemon juice

1½ cups heavy cream
2 tbsp. chopped parsley
3 tbsp. butter
Salt and pepper to taste

nappe: the consistency at which a liquid or sauce is thick enough to coat the back of a spoon

Méthode:
Blanch watercress, squeeze dry, and finely chop; set aside. Combine wine, garlic, and lemon juice in a large saucepot over medium heat and reduce by half. Add cream and reduce to nappe, the consistency of syrup. Combine watercress, parsley, and cream mixture in a blender; add butter slowly. Season with salt and pepper to taste. Serve over Frog Legs Provençale.

          CAFÉ DEGAS COOKBOOK

fumet: a fish and shellfish
stock

STEAMED DEGAS MUSSELS
Serves 6

3 lb. fresh mussels, thoroughly
  cleaned
2 tbsp. olive oil
1 fennel bulb, core removed,
  julienned
1 bunch leeks, sliced, white
  part only
1 onion, sliced
1 tbsp. sliced garlic
1 bouquet garni (thyme, bay,
  and parsley)

1 cup white wine
3 oz. orange juice
2 oz. lemon juice
2 cups water or fumet
1 oz. Herbsaint
4 sprigs fresh soft herbs (basil,
  tarragon, and cilantro)
Salt and pepper to taste
1 tbsp. unsalted butter

Méthode:
Combine all ingredients in a heavy pot and cover. Heat over high
heat, shaking pan occasionally until mussels open. Serve with
fresh French bread to mop up the delicious sauce and garnish
with Roasted Garlic Aïoli and Pomme Frites (see index).

PATÉ *de* CAMPAGNE (COUNTRY PATÉ)

Serves 25

2½ lb. country pork ribs
1 lb. duck livers
½ lb. fatback
2 cups mirepoix
2 garlic cloves, minced
1 tbsp. thyme
2 bay leaves
1 tbsp. combined pink and
   kosher salt

1 tbsp. freshly ground black
   pepper
¼ cup brandy
¼ cup all-purpose flour
1 egg
Caul fat (available at specialty
   butchers)

Méthode:

Debone the ribs and clean the livers. In a bowl, season ribs, livers, and fatback with mirepoix, garlic, thyme, bay leaves, salt, and pepper. Mix thoroughly and then cover in brandy. Marinate overnight then grind together (discarding bay leaves before grinding). Mix in the flour and egg. Remove to terrine, cover in caul fat, and bake uncovered for 1½ hours. Serve with your favorite crackers or baguette and garnish with cornichons.

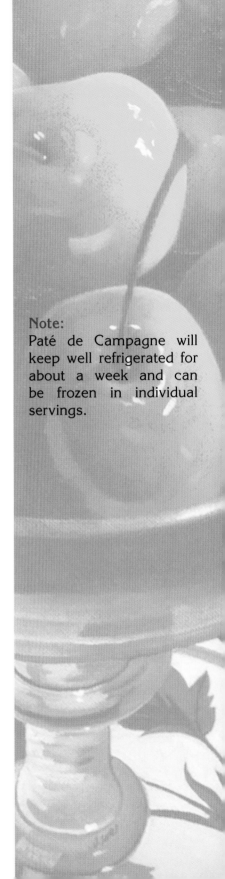

Note:
Paté de Campagne will keep well refrigerated for about a week and can be frozen in individual servings.

SALMON MOUSSE
Serves 4-6

1 lb. fresh salmon, poached
1 egg
1 cup heavy cream

Salt and white pepper to taste
Cornichons, capers, or local
   greens for garnish

Méthode:
Fill the bowl of a food processor with ice and refrigerate until chilled. Ice salmon to chill. Discard ice and combine salmon and egg in cold food processor and blend until they combine. Pour the cream into the processor in one motion. Blend as little as possible to distribute, remove from food processor, and refrigerate immediately. Refrigerate until ready to serve. Serve with a sliced baguette and Roasted Garlic Aïoli (see index). Garnish with cornichons, capers, or local greens.

SALMON *and* SMOKED TROUT RILLETTE
Serves 6-8

1 lb. salmon, poached
2 tbsp. shallots, sautéed
1 tsp. tarragon, minced
1 tbsp. salt
1 tsp. black pepper
1 tbsp. vodka
Juice from 1 lemon

1 oz. smoked trout, minced
1 tbsp. minced chives
1 cup whipping cream
4 tbsp. butter, melted
Cornichons or grapes for
  garnish

Méthode:
With a fork, flake poached salmon into a bowl resting in ice. Add the next eight ingredients and adjust seasoning. In a separate bowl whip cream to stiff peaks and fold into salmon mixture. Portion into small dishes or ramekins and cover with a thin layer of melted butter. Chill at least 4 hours. Serve as a spread with warm baguette slices. Garnish with cornichons or grapes.

RILLETTE *of* SUCKLING PIG
Serves 20

3 jalapenos	1 4-5-lb. pork butt
10 cloves garlic	2 tbsp. chopped thyme plus
¼ cup olive oil	5 sprigs
Zest of 1 orange	6 pt. chicken stock
Juice of 1 orange	¼ cup finely minced shallots
Salt and pepper to taste	¼ cup Dijon mustard

Méthode:

Blend or process jalapenos, garlic, olive oil, zest and juice, and a pinch of salt and pepper. Marinate pork in the jalapeno mixture for at least 4 hours. Remove pork from marinade and place pork in a brazier. Place in oven at 350 degrees for 10-15 minutes or until it achieves a light brown color. Add chicken stock and 3 thyme sprigs. Cover and cook in oven for about 4 hours at 300 degrees until pork falls apart. Remove from oven and pour liquid into a saucepan. Add shallots, Dijon mustard, and thyme to liquid. Reduce liquid over medium-low heat until it reaches nappe, or the consistency of syrup. Allow to cool and then cube pork or break meat into 2" sections. Drizzle with the sauce and serve.

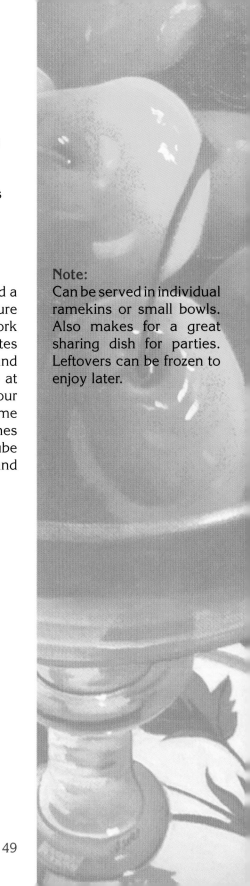

Note:
Can be served in individual ramekins or small bowls. Also makes for a great sharing dish for parties. Leftovers can be frozen to enjoy later.

MARINATED ARTICHOKES
Serves 6

6 baby artichokes, cleaned
1 tbsp. salt
Juice of 2 lemons
1 cup $^{8}\!/\!_{20}$ olive oil/vegetable
   oil

2 tbsp. chopped garlic
1 tsp. red pepper flakes
2 sprigs mint

Méthode:
Steam or boil artichokes with salt and lemon juice. Combine oil, garlic, red pepper, and mint in a bowl; add artichokes. Marinate for at least 2 hours or overnight in a refrigerator. Serve as a side to fish or as an appetizer with Roasted Garlic Aïoli (see index).

CRAWFISH PIE
Serves 4-6

¼ cup diced onion
¼ cup diced red pepper
2 tbsp. diced celery
2 tbsp. butter, divided
¼ cup fresh corn
2 tsp. sugar, optional
½ cup quartered mushrooms
½ cup Louisiana crawfish tails

1 tsp. chopped garlic
1 dash Tabasco or Crystal hot
   sauce
1 dash Worcestershire sauce
1 tbsp. brandy
¼ cup heavy cream
1 tbsp. chopped parsley
Salt and pepper to taste

Méthode:
Sauté onion, pepper, and celery (the Cajun "trinity") in 1 tbsp. butter until translucent. Remove to a bowl. Increase heat and sauté corn until bright yellow. Add 2 tsp. sugar or to taste. Add 1 tbsp. butter and the mushrooms to pan and, without shaking the mushrooms, sear until nicely browned. Remove to bowl with sautéed "trinity." Gently sauté crawfish tails with garlic until just heated through. Season with hot sauce and Worcestershire sauce. Add brandy away from heat and carefully flame. Transfer contents of the bowl to the pan with crawfish. Add heavy cream and parsley; simmer until thickened. Season with salt and pepper to taste. Serve in individual puff pastry cups or small pie shells.

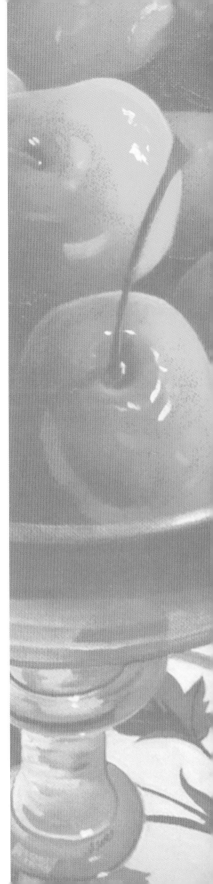

Soupes

LA GRATINÉE D'OIGNONS (ONION SOUP)
Serves 6-8

2 slices bacon, julienned
1 tbsp. butter
2 cloves garlic, sliced
3 medium onions, sliced
1 cup white wine
1 small bouquet garni
1 bay leaf

1 cup chicken stock
1 cup beef stock
1 tbsp. thyme
½ tsp. black pepper
½ tbsp. salt
Toasted baguette slices and
   Gruyère for garnish

Méthode:

In a large pot over low heat, render bacon in butter, allowing the fat to coat the bottom of the pot. Add garlic and simmer lightly. Add a quarter of the onions and cook, stirring until lightly browned. Deglaze with white wine. Add remaining onions, bouquet garni, bay leaf, and stock and cook, stirring occasionally, for 1 hour. Add remaining ingredients and cook for 3 hours or until onions are very tender. To serve, place one slice of the toasted baguette on top of each bowl of soup and then drizzle a generous amount of cheese to cover. If desired, broil for 1 minute to melt and brown the cheese.

bouquet garni: a gathering of fresh or dried herbs—generally parsley, bay leaf, thyme, and sometimes celery stalk—tied together with string and used to flavor broths, stews, and soups. The bouquet is always removed before serving.

VICHYSSOISE *with* DRIZZLED TRUFFLE OIL
Serves 8-10

1 bunch leeks, white part only, chopped
1 cup chopped onions
1 tbsp. chopped garlic
2 tbsp. butter
1 bay leaf
1 bouquet garni
1½ cups white wine
1 qt. chicken stock

3 Idaho potatoes, peeled and diced
2 cups heavy cream
2 tsp. salt
1 tsp. white pepper
Chives for garnish
Truffle oil
Snipped chives for garnish

Méthode:
Sweat leek, onion, and garlic in butter in a covered pot over low heat. Add bay leaf, bouquet, and white wine; reduce by half. Add chicken stock and potatoes and cook for 30 minutes or until potatoes are soft. Remove from heat and cool slightly. Puree liquid in a blender then strain through a fine mesh sieve. Mix cream into strained liquid until it achieves a creamy consistency. Season with salt and pepper to taste. Refrigerate and serve cold in chilled bowls. Drizzle truffle oil on top and garnish with snipped chives.

CARROT VICHYSSOISE

Serves 6

2 tbsp. extra-virgin olive oil
1 leek, sliced into rounds
½ Spanish onion, sliced
1 rib celery, chopped
1 tsp. chopped garlic
4 carrots, peeled and chopped
1 Russet potato, peeled and
  diced

4 cups chicken stock
1 bay leaf
2 tbsp. orange blossom water
¼ cup heavy cream
Salt and pepper to taste
2 tbsp. chives, thinly sliced or
  2 chive blossoms, whole

Méthode:
In a large saucepan over medium heat, add olive oil. When hot add leek, onion, celery, and garlic; cook for 5 minutes or until the vegetables are very tender. Add carrots, potato, chicken stock, and bay leaf. Cook for 35-40 minutes. Remove from heat and cool slightly. Puree in a blender then strain through a fine mesh sieve. Season with salt and pepper. Add orange blossom water and heavy cream. Simmer for 10 minutes. Chill and serve cold garnished with chives.

SWEET POTATO VICHYSSOISE
Serves 6

2 small sweet potatoes
1 small leek, chopped
1 tbsp. chopped garlic
1 cup chopped Spanish onion
2 tbsp. butter
1 bay leaf
1 small bouquet garni
½ cup white wine

1 qt. chicken or shrimp stock
1 cup heavy cream
2 cups milk
2 tsp. salt
½ tbsp. white pepper
½ lb. boiled shrimp for garnish
Chives for garnish

Méthode:

Bake sweet potatoes at 425 degrees until soft (about 1 hour); peel, quarter, and set aside. Sweat leek, garlic, and onion in butter over low heat in a covered pan until translucent. Add bay leaf, bouquet, and white wine; reduce by half. Add stock and simmer for 15 minutes. Add roasted sweet potatoes and bring to a boil. Remove from heat and cool. Puree in a blender then strain through a fine mesh sieve. Thoroughly mix in fresh cream and milk and season with salt and pepper to taste. Chill the soup. Serve cold and garnish with boiled shrimp and lots of snipped chives.

ITALIAN WEDDING SOUP
Serves 10

1 whole chicken
4 onions, chopped, divided
3-4 carrots, chopped, divided
½ bunch celery, diced, divided
2 tbsp. thyme
2 tbsp. fresh black pepper, divided
10 cloves garlic, whole
1 bunch leeks
20 cloves garlic, smashed
½ cup butter
½ cup extra-virgin olive oil
4 pt. diced tomatoes
1 tbsp. saffron
2 tbsp. ground cumin
½ bunch fresh parsley, chopped
½ bunch fresh spinach, julienned
Orzo pasta for garnish

Méthode:

To poach the chicken: rinse the chicken and place in a large pot. Cover with cold water. Add 2 chopped onions, 2 carrots, half of the celery, thyme, 1 tbsp. black pepper, and whole garlic. Bring to a brisk boil. Boil steadily for 10 minutes, stirring the pot to cook evenly. Remove from heat and cover. Let cool for 1 hour. Once cool, remove the chicken from the pot, reserving stock. Debone chicken and add bones to stock. Return to a boil and reduce by half. While stock is boiling, pull the chicken meat into small pieces; set aside. Once the stock is reduced, remove and discard the bones.

For the soup: sweat the leek, 2 onions, and smashed garlic in butter and olive oil in a covered pot over low heat. Add chicken stock, remaining celery, remaining carrots, diced tomato, saffron, cumin, and 1 tbsp. pepper. Simmer until everything is soft. Add chicken meat and chopped parsley; season to taste.

Serve over orzo pasta and garnish with fresh spinach.

GAZPACHO
Serves 6-8

2 cucumbers, peeled and
   chopped
2 celery stalks, chopped
1 red bell pepper, stemmed,
   seeded, and chopped
1 green bell pepper, stemmed,
   seeded, and chopped

4 tomatoes, crushed
Juice of 1 lime
¼ cup chopped red onion
2 cloves garlic, crushed
1 tbsp. chopped basil
1 qt. tomato juice
3 tbsp. sherry vinegar

Méthode:
Combine all ingredients and marinate for 24-48 hours. Puree.
Refrigerate until cold and serve.

ROASTED EGGPLANT *and* TOMATO SOUP
Serves 6

½ large onion, diced
1 carrot, diced
1 stalk celery, diced
1 lb. mushrooms, cleaned and
    quartered; stems included
10 cloves garlic, chopped,
    divided
2 tbsp. olive oil (not extra
    virgin)
Kosher salt or sea salt to taste
Black pepper to taste

1 cup dry white wine
1 medium eggplant, peeled
5 fresh or 1 qt. canned
    tomatoes, sliced
2 tbsp. chopped fresh parsley,
    chopped
1½ tsp. minced fresh thyme
1½ tsp. minced rosemary
2 bay leaves
Parmesan to garnish

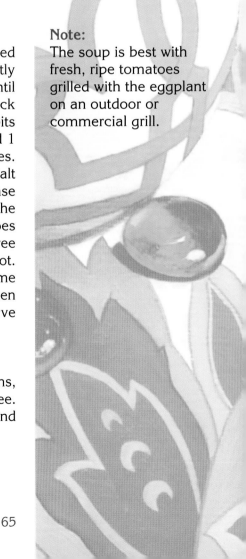

Note:
The soup is best with fresh, ripe tomatoes grilled with the eggplant on an outdoor or commercial grill.

Méthode:

Place onion, carrot, celery, mushrooms, and 5 cloves chopped garlic in a roasting pan. Drizzle liberally with olive oil, then lightly season with salt and pepper. Roast, stirring occasionally, until the vegetables turn golden brown. Remove vegetables to a stock pot, then deglaze the roasting pan with wine, scraping any bits from the bottom. Pour into the pot and cover with water; add 1 qt. additional water. Bring to a boil then simmer for 45 minutes. While mushroom stock is boiling, peel and slice eggplant. Salt each side and let rest in a colander to drain for 20 minutes. Rinse under cool water and squeeze out excess moisture. Drizzle the eggplant with olive oil then grill or roast eggplant and tomatoes until soft, rubbing with chopped garlic once cooked. Puree eggplant and tomatoes; set aside. Strain stock then return to pot. Add eggplant-tomato puree, chopped parsley, minced thyme and rosemary, bay leaves, and 1 qt. water. Bring to a boil then simmer for 45 minutes. Refrigerate overnight, reheat, and serve with Parmesan dusted on top.

Alternatif:

For a shortcut, roast everything (onion, carrot, celery, mushrooms, garlic, eggplant, and tomatoes) then deglaze with wine; puree. Simmer with 1 cup store-bought vegetable or chicken stock and herbs. Serve immediately or let the flavors melds overnight.

MIRLITON, SHRIMP, *and* CRAB BISQUE
Serves 8-10

¾ cup butter
1½ cups all-purpose flour
1 stick of celery, diced
1 large onion, peeled and diced
1 large carrot, peeled and diced
¾ cup Sauterne wine
2½ qt. hot water
¼ cup crab base

2 tbsp. liquid crab boil
1 qt. heavy cream
4 mirlitons, peeled and diced to ¼"
2 bay leaves
1 lb. fresh Louisiana brown shrimp, peeled
½ lb. fresh Louisiana blue crab claws or crabmeat
Salt and white pepper to taste

Méthode:
Melt the butter and then stir in flour. Cook, stirring, for 5 minutes over medium-low heat to achieve a nice white roux. Add celery, onion, and carrot and cook for an additional 5 minutes, stirring constantly. Pour in Sauterne and whisk until the roux is dissolved completely in the mixture. Add hot water, crab base, and crab boil and whisk until the base is dissolved. Bring to a boil and simmer for 15 minutes. Strain through a chinois and discard solids. Add the heavy cream, mirlitons, and bay leaves. Cook until the mirlitons are tender. Stir in the brown shrimp and crab claws 5 minutes before serving. Season with salt and white pepper to taste.

SOUPE *de* MELON
Serves 6-8

4 lb. cantaloupe or honeydew melons	3 tbsp. sugar
Zest of 1 lemon	2 qt. whole milk
1 sprig mint leaves	3 oz. port
	1 tsp. cinnamon

Méthode:
Peel the melon and then cut half of the melon into balls. Dice the remainder of the melon. Cook the milk, sugar and port over medium to low heat for 20 minutes. Allow to cool for about ten minutes. Pour into blender, add the diced melons and mix. Pass it through a china cap. Add half of the lemon zest and chopped mint. Remove to a large bowl and allow to sit overnight in the refrigerator. To serve, place a few melon balls into chilled bowls, ladle out the cold soup. Garnish with the mint leaves and zest. Enjoy on a hot south Louisiana afternoon.

CUCUMBER SOUP
Serves 4-6

4 large cucumbers, peeled
  and chopped, divided
1 qt. half-and-half
1 pt. heavy cream
1 green onion stalk, diced
2 sprigs dill weed
2 cloves garlic, finely chopped

½ cup diced green peppers
¼ cup iceberg lettuce,
  chopped
2 cups sour cream
6 sprigs parsley
Salt and white pepper to taste

Méthode:

Reserving one cucumber and 1 cup sour cream, combine all ingredients in a large bowl. Add in batches to a blender and mix thoroughly to fully blend the components. Mix in salt and white pepper to taste. Refrigerate until cold. Serve in chilled bowls and garnished with finely diced cucumber and a dollop of sour cream.

Salades

WHITE BEAN *and* DUCK CONFIT SALAD
Serves 6

6 duck legs
1 tbsp. Kosher salt
1 tbsp. black pepper
6 sprigs thyme
1 tbsp. nutmeg
1 tbsp. cumin
1 tbsp. cinnamon
1 tbsp. coriander
12 garlic cloves, finely
  chopped

6 bay leaves, ground or
  chopped
2 lb. white beans
$\frac{8}{20}$ blended olive oil/
  vegetable oil
½ cup chopped carrot
½ cup chopped onion
½ cup chopped green onion
½ chopped cup celery
1 tbsp. butter

Méthode:
Rub the duck legs with salt, black pepper, spices, garlic, and bay leaves. Allow to cure for 24 hours in the refrigerator. Soak the white beans in water for 24 hours. After the duck has cured, baste with $\frac{8}{20}$ olive oil/vegetable oil and bake for 5 hours at 275 degrees. Remove from oven and shred the meat from the bones. Set aside. Lightly simmer the carrot, onion, green onion, and celery with butter in a large pot for 5 minutes. Mix in the white beans and water to cover. Cook for 25 minutes over medium heat or until beans are tender. Drain and cool. Mix the duck and beans together and toss with Balsamic Vinaigrette, Black Pepper Vinaigrette, or Degas Dijon Vinaigrette (see index).

BRUSSELS SPROUT SALAD
Serves 4

2 lb. Brussels sprouts
4 slices thick-cut bacon, cut
    into small pieces
1 red onion, thinly sliced

2 tsp. chopped fresh mint
2 tsp. chopped tarragon
Stilton cheese for garnish

Méthode:
Remove the tough outer layers from the Brussels sprouts and slice in half. In a large pot of boiling, salted water, cook sprouts for 2-3 minutes until just tender. Immediately remove from boiling water and submerge in a bowl of ice water. Once cool, remove the Brussels sprouts to a sheet pan lined with a paper towel to drain. While the sprouts are draining, in a medium sauté pan over low heat render the bacon until crisp. Remove the bacon and set aside. Add the Brussels sprouts to the pan and cook in bacon fat until light brown. Remove to a bowl. Toss the Brussels sprouts with red onion and bacon. Add Vinaigrette and sprinkle with chopped herbs. Serve warm garnished with crumbled Stilton cheese.

VINAIGRETTE
Makes 2 cups

½ cup sherry vinegar
½ cup corn syrup
1 cup olive oil

Salt and pepper to taste
¼ lb. Stilton cheese, crumbled

Méthode:
In a small mixing bowl, mix sherry vinegar with corn syrup. Slowly add the olive oil in a steady stream. Season with salt and pepper and gently toss with Stilton cheese. Serve over Brussels Sprout Salad.

SALADE NIÇOISE
Serves 6

6 generous handfuls of fresh
   spring greens
18 Marinated Niçoise Olives
   (recipe follows)
1 red onion, thinly sliced
12 green beans, steamed
3 potatoes, cooked, peeled,
   and quartered

3 Louisiana Creole tomatoes
6 eggs, boiled and halved
4 oz. yellowfin tuna filet
1 tsp. 80/20 blended olive oil/
   vegetable oil
6 anchovy filets

Méthode:
Place greens in 6 separate bowls and divide olives, red onion, green beans, potatoes, tomatoes, and halved eggs evenly among the bowls. Dress with Degas Dijon Vinaigrette. Heat oil in a skillet. Sear tuna 3 minutes on each side or to preferred doneness. Slice and set hot tuna onto each of the salads and finish by placing an anchovy atop the tuna.

DEGAS DIJON VINAIGRETTE
Yields 1 qt.

2 egg yolks
2 tsp. chopped garlic
1 tbsp. chopped shallots
2 tbsp. Dijon mustard
½ cup red wine vinegar

1½ cups olive oil
1½ cups canola oil
1 tsp. salt
1 tsp. pepper
1 tbsp. honey

Méthode:
Whisk first 5 ingredients together. Slowly whisk in oils. Add remaining ingredients. Serve over Salade Niçoise and other fresh salads.

MARINATED NIÇOISE OLIVES
Makes 1 gal.

1 gal. black olives, drained
  and rinsed
¼ cup sliced garlic
¼ cup sliced shallots
4 sprigs rosemary, chopped
4 sprigs thyme, chopped
2 tbsp. ground fennel

2 tbsp. ground coriander
2 bay leaves
2 tbsp. crushed black
  peppercorns
1 tsp. ground cumin
1 tsp. chili flakes
4 cups olive oil

Méthode:
In a large bowl combine olives with garlic, shallots, rosemary, and thyme; set aside Toast spices in a small pan over medium heat until aromatic. Add oil and simmer 5 minutes. Strain oil over olives and allow to cool. Serve with Salade Niçoise or other dishes calling for olives.

LA SALADE *de* CHÈVRE TIÈDE
Serves 1

1 beet, peeled and sliced
⁸⁰⁄₂₀ blended olive oil/
    vegetable oil
Salt and pepper to taste
2 sprigs rosemary
7 roasted walnuts

Generous handful of fresh
    mixed greens
1 Granny Smith apple, sliced
    into sixths
2 baguette slices, toasted
1 tbsp. goat cheese

Méthode:
Place beets in an oven-safe dish then drizzle with oil. Season with salt and pepper to taste. Place rosemary atop beets. Cover with tin foil and cook at 350 degrees for 2 hours. While beets are cooking, arrange walnuts in a second oven-safe dish and bake at 350 degrees for 10-15 minutes. In a bowl, toss mixed greens with Balsamic Vinaigrette. Arrange cooked beets over the greens in a pattern with the apple slices. Add walnuts. Slather the baguette slices with goat cheese. Warm the bread in an oven for 5 minutes at 200 degrees. Serve with salad and enjoy.

BALSAMIC VINAIGRETTE
Yields 1 qt.

½ cup balsamic vinegar
¼ cup minced shallots
2 tbsp. Dijon mustard
2 tsp. minced garlic
3 cups olive oil

1 tbsp. salt
1 tsp. freshly ground black
    pepper
3 tbsp. honey

Méthode:
Whisk together first 4 ingredients. Slowly whisk in oil. Mix in remaining ingredients. Serve over your favorite fresh salad. Saves well when refrigerated.

PARMESAN- *and* PANKO-CRUSTED SOFT-SHELL CRAB SALAD

Serves 6

6 fresh large Louisiana soft-shell crabs
Kosher salt and freshly ground black pepper to taste
2 cups flour
3 eggs
1 cup breadcrumbs

½ cup Panko
2 tbsp. grated Parmesan
1 tbsp. chopped fresh parsley
½ cup olive oil
3 tbsp. butter
6 oz. baby lettuces
Bulgarian feta cheese

Méthode:

Clean crabs and season with salt and pepper. Pour flour into a bowl. In a separate bowl, beat eggs. In a third bowl, combine breadcrumbs and Panko with Parmesan, parsley, and salt and pepper. Dredge crabs in flour then wash in eggs. Dredge crabs in the breadcrumb mixture twice to ensure they are thickly coated. Heat oil and butter in a large sauté pan until just below the smoking point. Add crabs 2 at a time (be very careful not to overcrowd the pan and splash the oil). Fry until lightly brown on both sides and transfer to a paper towel to drain. Toss baby lettuces with Black Pepper Vinaigrette and garnish with Pickled Red Onions and feta.

Alternatif:

Following the recipe above, substitute oysters for soft-shell crabs.

BLACK PEPPER VINAIGRETTE
Makes 1 qt.

2 tbsp. minced shallot
1 tbsp. Dijon mustard
2 tbsp. freshly ground black
   pepper
¼ cup honey

1 tbsp. minced tarragon
½ cup red wine vinegar
½ cups $^{80}/_{20}$ blended olive oil/
   vegetable oil
1 tsp. kosher salt

Méthode:
Combine all ingredients except oil and salt. Slowly whisk in oil and salt. Serve with Parmesan- and Panko-Crusted Soft-Shell Crab Salad. Saves well when refrigerated.

PICKLED RED ONIONS

1 cup red wine vinegar
1 tbsp. honey
1 tbsp. sugar

1 jalapeno, sliced
2 red onions, sliced into
   ½" segments

Méthode:
In a small saucepan, bring vinegar, honey, sugar, and jalapeno to a boil. Boil for 1 minute. Pour mixture over red onions and allow to marinate in refrigerator overnight. Once the onions have marinated, strain onions from marinade and set aside. Heat marinade over medium-high heat. Reduce to a light syrup. Pour over onions and allow to cool. Serve with Parmesan- and Panko-Crusted Soft-Shell Crab Salad.

CRAB SALAD *with* ORANGE-DIJON VINAIGRETTE
Serves 4-6

1 lb. jumbo lump Louisiana
   crabmeat
1 fennel bulb, julienned

2 grapefruits
Salt and pepper to taste
2 oz. baby arugula

Méthode:
Carefully clean and pick crabmeat, keeping lumps whole. Peel and supreme (segment) grapefruit and set aside. Toss crabmeat with Orange-Dijon Vinaigrette; season with salt and pepper. Place crabmeat atop bed of arugula, garnish with grapefruit, and top with Orange-Dijon Vinaigrette.

ORANGE-DIJON VINAIGRETTE
Makes 1 qt.

¾ cup cane vinegar
¼ cup finely chopped shallots
1 tbsp. finely chopped garlic
¼ cup chopped tarragon
1 tbsp. finely chopped fresh
   thyme

1 tbsp. Dijon mustard
¼ cup orange zest
¼ cup fresh orange juice
3 cups $^{80}/_{20}$ blended olive oil/
   vegetable oil
Salt and pepper to taste

Méthode:
Combine all ingredients except the oil and whisk together. Slowly add oil to emulsify. Season with salt and pepper to taste. Serve over Crab Salad. Saves well when refrigerated.

CABBAGE SLAW
Serves 10

⅔ cup apple cider vinegar
½ cup sugar
1 jalapeno, seeded and
   minced
3 tbsp. diced parsley

1 cup olive oil
6-8 carrots, shredded
1 head cabbage, shredded
Salt and pepper to taste

Méthode:
Whisk together vinegar and sugar. Add jalapeno, parsley, and olive oil; mix well. Toss shredded carrots and cabbage with salt and pepper then add jalapeno, parsley, and olive oil. Marinate overnight.

Alternatif:
Shredded jicama may be added to this dish for a refreshing twist.

LOUISIANA CREOLE TOMATO SALAD *with* RICOTTA CHEESE

Serves 4

2 large, ripe Creole tomatoes, chilled
½ cup chopped fresh basil
1 tbsp. dried oregano

1 cup grated ricotta cheese
¼ cup extra-virgin olive oil
¼ cup balsamic vinegar

Méthode:
Thickly slice the tomatoes and evenly divide slices among 4 salad plates. Sprinkle 2 tbsp. fresh basil and ¾ tsp. oregano over tomatoes on each plate. Top with ¼ cup grated ricotta cheese. Drizzle with 1 tbsp. each of the olive oil and balsamic vinegar. Serve.

Alternatif:
Replace the oil and vinegar with Degas Dijon Vinaigrette (see index).

FRIED GARLIC VINAIGRETTE
1 qt.

½ cup sliced garlic
3 cups olive oil
2 egg yolks
2 tbsp. Dijon mustard

¼ cup sherry vinegar
½ cup minced parsley
½ cup water, optional

Méthode:
Fry sliced garlic in olive oil until golden brown, drain, and reserve oil. Combine next 4 ingredients in blender, mix for 30 seconds, and emulsify with reserved olive oil. Add water to thin to desired consistency if necessary. Stir in fried garlic. Serve over your favorite fresh salad. Saves well when refrigerated.

RASPBERRY VINAIGRETTE
Yields approximately 1 qt.

1 tbsp. minced shallots
1 tsp. minced garlic
1 cup raspberry vinegar
1½ tbsp. Dijon mustard

1 egg yolk
1½ cups olive oil
2 tbsp. sugar

Méthode:
Whisk together first 5 ingredients. Slowly whisk in oil then whisk in sugar. Chill. Serve over your favorite fresh salad. Saves well when refrigerated.

AVOCADO DRESSING

Yields approximately 1 qt.

3 avocadoes, peeled and
  diced
2 tsp. garlic
2 tbsp. lime juice
1 tbsp. sherry vinegar

½ cup tomato juice
1½ cups olive oil
2 tsp. salt
1 tsp. pepper

Méthode:
Puree avocadoes with garlic, lime juice, and vinegar. Add tomato juice. In a slow, steady stream, add olive oil to emulsify. Season with salt and pepper. Serve over your favorite fresh salad. Saves well when refrigerated.

CITRUS SESAME VINAIGRETTE
Yields approximately 1 qt.

¼ cup black sesame seeds
Juice of 2 limes
Zest of 1 lime
Juice of 2 satsumas

Juice of 2 lemons
¾ cup corn syrup
½ cup orange juice

Méthode:
Gently whisk all ingredients together. Chill. Serve over your favorite fresh salad. Saves well when refrigerated.

SHERRY VINAIGRETTE
Yields 3 cups

1 cup sherry vinegar
1 cup corn syrup
1 cup $^{80}\!/_{20}$ blended olive oil/
   vegetable oil

Salt and pepper to taste

Méthode:
Combine all with hand blender. Season to taste. Serve over your favorite fresh salad. Saves well when refrigerated.

GREEN OLIVE MARINADE
Makes 1 gal.

8 tbsp. finely chopped garlic
1 cup olive oil
1 tbsp. finely chopped
  rosemary
2 tbsp. finely chopped fresh
  thyme
1 tbsp. finely chopped fresh
  parsley

¼ cup red wine vinegar
3 tbsp. finely chopped shallots
1 tbsp. salt
1 tsp. pepper
1 gal. green (or Spanish)
  olives, drained and rinsed

Méthode:
Toast garlic in olive oil until lightly brown and aromatic. Add herbs and remove from heat. When cool, whisk herbed oil into vinegar. Add shallots and season with salt and pepper. In a large bowl, marinate olives in oil overnight. Serve with your favorite fresh salad or other dishes calling for green olives.

SPICED PECANS
Makes 1 lb.

1 lb. Louisiana pecans halves
6 tbsp. sugar
½ cup butter

2 tbsp. Worcestershire sauce
1 tsp. cayenne pepper
1 tbsp. salt

Méthode:
Combine all ingredients, mixing and coating pecans thoroughly. Toast on parchment paper in a 350-degree oven for 25-30 minutes, turning as needed until done. Cool in a single layer. Serve as a great addition to your favorite fresh salad.

Sauces

demi-glace: a reduction of brown stock, espagnole sauce, and bouquet garni

BLACK MISSION FIGS *with* PORT REDUCTION SAUCE
Makes about 1 cup

1 cup port
2 small shallots, minced
½ cup veal demi-glace (available at specialty markets and in powdered form)

Fresh ground black pepper to taste
12 black mission figs
6 oz. Stilton, Roquefort, or your favorite strong blue cheese

Méthode:
Combine port with shallots and cook over high heat until reduced to about ½ cup liquid. Add demi-glace and reduce to a velvety consistency. Add black pepper to taste, just enough to complement the savory aspects of the port. Serve over halved, ripe black mission figs and blue cheese. An excellent addition to duck, pork, or lamb.

BÉCHAMEL
Makes about 1 cup

¼ cup chopped celery
1 tbsp. chopped garlic
2 tbsp. butter
2 tbsp. flour

½ cup whole milk
1 bay leaf
1 tbsp. ground clove nutmeg
½ cup grated Gruyère or Swiss

Méthode:
Sweat celery and garlic in butter in a covered pan over low heat. Add flour and cook until lightly browned. Mix in milk, bay leaf, and clove nutmeg and cook gently until thickened. Serve over cauliflower, asparagus, or broccoli as a side dish. Top with grated Swiss or Gruyère and broil for 2-3 minutes to melt cheese to a golden color.

Alternatif:
An interesting and flavorful derivation of the traditional béchamel can be achieved by cooking ½ cup chopped leeks with the celery and garlic.

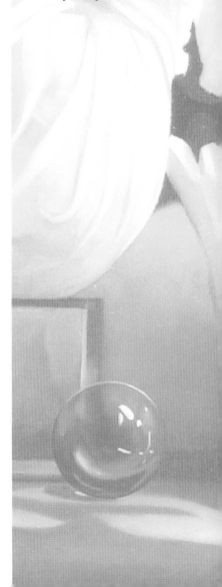

béchamel: a sauce thickened by a roux and flavored with onion, cloves, and bay leaf

Note:
This traditional béchamel works well with most savory crêpes.

compote: fruit stewed with sugar

CIPOLLINI COMPOTE
Makes about 1 cup

½ cup white wine
½ cup balsamic vinegar
½ stick cinnamon
½ star anise seed
1 tbsp. chopped fresh ginger
1 piece lemongrass
2 whole peppercorns

¼ cup sugar
1 sprig rosemary
1 cup duck or chicken stock
6-8 black mission figs
8-10 cipollini, peeled (may
    substitute with 2 Vidalia
    onions, chopped)

Méthode:
Combine wine, vinegar, cinnamon, anise, ginger, lemongrass, peppercorns, sugar, and rosemary in a large pot. Over high heat, reduce to 1½ cups. Add stock and reduce mixture to half. Cover cipollini and figs with stock mixture and braise until cipollini bulbs pop out. Pour sauce over figs and refrigerate. Serve cold over pork and lamb.

BALSAMIC REDUCTION
Yields 2 cups

½ cup chopped onion
¼ cup chopped celery
1 clove garlic, minced
¼ cup diced carrot
½ apple, peeled and quartered
1 tsp. olive oil

1 cup port wine
1 cup balsamic vinegar
1 cup veal glace
Salt to taste
Pinch sugar, optional

Méthode:
Slowly caramelize first 5 ingredients in olive oil over medium heat. Add port and reduce by half over medium-high heat. Add balsamic vinegar; reduce by half. Lower heat, then add veal glace and reduce slowly, skimming surface to remove fat, until it reaches nappe, a syrupy consistency. Strain through a fine mesh sieve. Season with salt. Correct acidity if necessary by adding a pinch of sugar. Serve over pork or fowl.

BEURRE ROUGE
Yields 2 cups

2 cups red wine
1 cup balsamic vinegar
1 tbsp. chopped garlic

½ cup heavy cream
2 lb. butter

Méthode:
Reduce wine, vinegar, and garlic until almost dry. Add cream and reduce until thick. Whisk in butter. Season with salt and pepper to taste. Serve over fish.

CHIMMICHURRI
Yields 2 cups

2 bunches cilantro, chopped
   with stems
1 bunch parsley, chopped
1 bunch scallions, chopped
½ jalapeno, chopped with
   seeds

Juice of 4 limes
1 tbsp. chopped garlic
1 tbsp. tarragon
Salt and pepper to taste
¾ cup olive oil

Méthode:
Combine all ingredients except olive oil in a food processor and process to a coarse texture. Slowly drizzle in olive oil to emulsify. Serve over your favorite cut of prepared beef.

DEGAS COCKTAIL SAUCE
Yields 1 cup

1 cup catsup
2 tbsp. horseradish
1 tsp. Worcestershire
¼ cup olive oil

2 tbsp. tarragon vinegar
1 tbsp. minced garlic
Salt and pepper to taste

Méthode:
Combine all ingredients. Let stand for 1 hour. Serve as a dipping sauce for shellfish.

au sec: cooking something down so far that it is nearly dry

LAMB SAUCE
Yields 1½ cups

¼ bottle merlot
1 shallot, sliced
2 whole peppercorns
1 bay leaf
1 bouquet garni

1 qt. lamb stock
1 tsp. sliced olives, plus olives
  for garnish
1 tsp. diced feta
1 tsp. diced tomatoes

Méthode:
Combine first 5 ingredients and reduce by half over medium heat. Add lamb stock and simmer, skimming to remove fat, until reduced by one-third. Pass sauce through a fine mesh sieve. Return sauce to pot, add sliced olives, and reduce until it becomes the consistency of a light syrup. Serve with rack of lamb or leg of lamb garnished with tomatoes, olives, and feta cheese.

MAÎTRE d'HOTEL BUTTER
Yields 1½ cups

¼ cup minced shallots
1 cup butter
2 tbsp. brandy
1 tbsp. minced garlic

¼ cup chopped fresh parsley
1½ tsp. salt
1½ tsp. black pepper

Méthode:
Sweat shallots in butter over low heat in a covered pan. Deglaze with brandy and let cool. Combine all ingredients in a blender and mix until smooth. Refrigerate. Form into cylinders by scooping out the semi-hardened mixture into a thick line onto cellophane sheets. Wrap with the cellophane and roll into long cylinders about the diameter of half dollars. Chill in ice water or Refrigerate. To serve, slice into small pads of butter and allow to melt over steak or escargot.

SUNDRIED TOMATO MARSALA SAUCE
Yields 1½ cups

½ cup small-diced pancetta
½ cup sliced shallots
½ cup sliced garlic
1 bay leaf
½ bottle Marsala

2 cups veal stock
¼ cup chopped sundried
  tomatoes
1 tbsp. rosemary
1 tbsp. thyme

Méthode:
Render pancetta slowly until nicely browned; drain almost all the fat. Add shallots, garlic, and bay leaf and sweat, covered, over low heat until cooked. Deglaze with Marsala and reduce by half over medium heat. Add veal stock and sundried tomatoes and reduce to nappe. Remove bay leaf. Finish with rosemary and thyme. Serve over veal or osso buco.

rouille: herb-infused garlic and oil used as a dip or spread on a baguette

ROUILLE
Makes about 1 cup

2 egg yolks
2 tsp. red wine vinegar
3 tsp. garlic
2 tsp. lemon juice
1 tsp. Dijon mustard

2 tsp. paprika
½ tsp. Sriracha sauce
¼ cup extra-virgin olive oil
2 tsp. salt
1 tsp. pepper

Méthode:
Blend first 7 ingredients in a food processor for 1 minute. Scrape sides and bottom well and process additional 30 seconds or until well combined. Slowly add oil to make a thick consistency for spreading. Add olive oil in slow, steady stream no thicker than a pencil lead. Add salt and pepper and process another 15 seconds. Refrigerate for 1 hour. Stir to combine before serving. Serve slathered over toasted baguette slices.

ROASTED GARLIC AÏOLI
Makes about 2 cups

2 egg yolks	1 tsp. Dijon mustard
2 tbsp. red wine vinegar	2 cups olive oil
2 tsp. minced garlic, roasted	2 tsp. salt
Juice of 1 lemon	1 tsp. pepper

Méthode:
Whisk first 5 ingredients together until well combined. Slowly whisk in oil to make thick emulsion. Stir in salt and pepper. Adjust seasoning. Serve over Steamed Degas Mussels.

Poissons

BOUILLABAISSE
Serves 6

1 fennel bulb, core removed and julienned
1 small leek, sliced (white part only)
½ cup sliced onions
1 tbsp. sliced garlic
1 bouquet garni
3 tbsp. olive oil
1 tsp. saffron
2 oz. Herbsaint

1 cup white wine
4 qt. shrimp stock or fumet
4 oz. fresh Louisiana brown shrimp (21-25 count per lb.), peeled and deveined, tails on
6 3-oz. Louisiana Redfish filets, skin on
8 oz. mussels, thoroughly cleaned

Méthode:
Sweat first 5 ingredients in olive oil over low heat until very tender. Add saffron and cook, stirring for 2 minutes, until saffron is well distributed. Deglaze with Herbsaint. Add wine and reduce by half. Add stock and cook for 15 minutes over medium heat. Add shrimp and fish and cover for 5 minutes. Add mussels and cook until mussels open, about 4 minutes. Serve with crusty baguette slices slathered with Rouille (see index).

SOUTH LOUISIANA CRAWFISH CRÊPES
Serves 4

FILLING

¼ cup diced onion
¼ cup diced green pepper
2 tbsp. diced celery
½ lb. Louisiana andouille
1 tbsp. butter
4 oz. Louisiana crawfish tails
1 tsp. chopped garlic

1 tsp. garlic
1 dash Tabasco or Crystal hot
 sauce
1 dash Worcestershire sauce
¼ cup heavy cream
1 tbsp. chopped parsley
Salt and pepper to taste

Méthode:

Sauté Cajun trinity (onion, pepper, and celery) and andouille in butter until vegetables are translucent. Remove to bowl. Gently sauté crawfish tails and garlic in andouille fat until just heated through. Season with hot sauce and Worcestershire sauce. Add contents of bowl to crawfish. Add heavy cream and parsley and simmer until thickened. Season with salt and pepper. Serve with Leek Béchamel (see index) over crêpes.

écrevisses: crawfish!

CRÊPES
Makes 8 crêpes

2 eggs	2 tbsp. butter, melted
⅓ cup flour	Pinch salt
½ cup milk	1 tsp sugar

Whisk or blend all ingredients until they reach a creamy consistency. Allow to rest at least 30 minutes or refrigerate overnight. Heat a skillet with butter over low to medium heat. Slowly ladle about ½ cup mixture into the pan, spreading as evenly and thinly as possible. Cook for 2-3 minutes, until small bubbles appear. Carefully turn crêpe with a spatula and cook an additional 30 seconds to 1 minute. Serve with both savory and sweet dishes.

CRÊPE DEGAS
Serves 4

2 tbsp. unsalted butter
½ lb. wild mushrooms
Salt and fresh ground pepper
   to taste
1 clove garlic, minced
2 tbsp. minced shallots

1 bunch asparagus, steamed
   and sliced thinly
1 lb. jumbo lump crabmeat
¼ cup brandy
Cayenne pepper to taste

Méthode:
In a medium sauté pan, melt butter and sauté mushrooms; season with salt and pepper. Reduce heat to low. Add garlic and shallots and sweat, covered, for 2 minutes. Fold in asparagus and crabmeat and flame with brandy; season with salt and pepper and a touch of cayenne. Wrap in Crêpe (see index) and top with Hollandaise Sauce. Broil each crêpe for 3-4 minutes to achieve a beautiful golden hue.

HOLLANDAISE SAUCE

3 egg yolks
2 tbsp. lemon juice
¼ tsp. salt

1 stick butter, melted
Freshly ground white pepper

Méthode:
In a blender, combine egg yolks, lemon juice, and salt. Blend on high for 30 seconds. While blending, add the butter in a slow, steady stream until the sauce thickens. Season with freshly ground pepper. Serve over Crêpes Degas.

CRAWFISH RÉMOULADE
Serves 6-8

½ cup Creole mustard
⅛ cup balsamic vinegar
¼ cup minced cornichons
2 tbsp. chopped capers
1 tbsp. minced garlic
3 tbsp. parsley
½ cup extra-virgin olive oil

½ cup Roasted Garlic Aïoli
  (see index)
¼ cup chopped garlic
¼ cup chopped shallot
4 tbsp. butter
2 lb. Louisiana crawfish tails
Salt and pepper to taste

Méthode:
Combine first 6 ingredients, then slowly whisk in olive oil. Stir in Aïoli. Refrigerate. In a large skillet, sauté garlic and shallot in butter. Add crawfish tails and sauté briefly, stirring occasionally. Toss with chilled rémoulade sauce and season with salt and pepper to taste. Serve cold over a bed of chopped greens.

SPICY RÉMOULADE

1 egg yolk
1 tbsp. chopped shallots
1 tbsp. chopped garlic
2 tsp. paprika
1 tsp. sambal olek
2 tbsp. chopped parsley
1 tbsp. red wine vinegar

2 tbsp. Creole mustard
2 tbsp. whole capers
2 tsp. horseradish
1½ cups olive oil
½ cup water, optional
½ tsp. salt
½ tsp. pepper

Méthode:
Combine first 10 ingredients in a blender and puree well, scraping sides. Slowly add olive oil, thinning with water if desired. Refrigerate. In a large skillet, sauté crawfish tails briefly, stirring occasionally. Toss with rémoulade and season with salt and pepper to taste. Serve cold over a bed of chopped greens.

DEGAS CRAWFISH *and* ANDOUILLE *over* EGGS
Serves 6-8

1 lb. andouille, chopped
3 red peppers, chopped
3 green peppers, chopped
1 onion, diced
2 tbsp. minced garlic
1 bay leaf
1 tbsp. thyme

2 fresh Creole tomatoes, diced
1 lb. crawfish
2 tbsp. butter
Salt and pepper to taste
1 tbsp. Worcestershire sauce
2 tsp. Tabasco or Crystal hot
   sauce

Méthode:

Sweat andouille, peppers, onion, and garlic in olive oil in a large rondeau over low heat. Add bay leaf and thyme. Puree tomatoes in a food processor and add to pepper mixture. Stirring continuously, cook 30 minutes. Remove from heat and cool. Sauté crawfish in small batches in butter with salt and pepper. Add to tomato mixture. Season with Worcestershire sauce and hot sauce. Serve over scrambled eggs or an omelet or serve with eggs inside a crêpe.

MARINATED GRILLED GULF SHRIMP *with* FRESH BASIL PESTO
Serves 8

4 tsp. cracked coriander
3 tsp. minced garlic
3 tsp. thyme
½ tsp. black pepper

Zest of 2 lemons
½ cup olive oil
4 lb. Louisiana brown shrimp, skewered

Méthode:
Combine all ingredients except shrimp. Brush mixture evenly over skewered shrimp. Place on medium-hot grill for no more than 5 minutes, turning once and reapplying marinade. Shrimp are done when they turn pink. Serve with Fresh Basil Pesto over orzo, rice, basmati, or grits.

FRESH BASIL PESTO

2 garlic cloves
1½ cups olive oil, divided
Juice of 1 lemon
1 tsp. salt
1 cup packed fresh basil,
    stems removed

1 cup packed fresh spinach,
    stems removed
¼ cup grated Parmesan
1 tbsp. chopped parsley
Salt and black pepper to taste

Méthode:
Place garlic cloves in a blender with ¼ cup olive oil. Puree briefly. Add lemon juice and salt. Finely chiffonade the basil and add to blender one small handful at a time. Puree. Scrape down sides of blender well. Continue process until all the basil has been well pureed. Add olive oil only as needed to keep the basil moving within the blender. If you add too much oil before the basil is thoroughly pureed, the basil will not break down properly. Once all basil has been pureed, add fine chiffonade of spinach by small handfuls. Add oil as needed, scraping down the sides of the blender. Add chopped parsley, Parmesan, and salt and pepper to taste. Serve over Marinated Grilled Gulf Shrimp.

SKATE *with* TOMATO PROVENÇALE
Serves 6

3 tomatoes
Salt and pepper to taste
1 tbsp. garlic, chopped
6 tbsp. olive oil
1 tbsp. crushed rosemary

1 tbsp. chopped thyme
1 tbsp. chopped parsley
6 3-5 oz. skate filets
2 tbsp. large caper berries

Méthode:
Core tomatoes and slice in half lengthwise; season with salt and pepper. Arrange in chafing dish then set aside. Toast garlic in olive oil until lightly browned and aromatic. Add remaining herbs and remove from heat. Spoon herb mixture over tomatoes, coating each tomato well. Roast tomatoes in the oven at 350 degrees for 15 minutes, basting occasionally, until tender. Arrange skate on top of each tomato and add caper berries. Cover with foil and finish in oven until skate pulls apart with a fork, about 15 minutes.

Alternatif:
Drum or monkfish can be substituted for skate.

court-bouillon: a vegetable- and herb-flavored broth primarily serving as a stock for seafood dishes

DRUM CROQUETTES *with* CHORIZO-STUFFED CREOLE TOMATOES
Serves 6-8

1 6-8 oz. red drum filet
Court-bouillon
½ cup diced onion
2 tsp. chopped garlic
4 tbsp. butter, divided
1 tsp. chopped fresh thyme
2 tbsp. fresh basil chiffonade

Juice of 1 lemon
2 tbsp. fish stock or fumet
2 anchovy filets, chopped
½ cup fresh breadcrumbs, divided
1 cup olive oil
Arugula to garnish

Méthode:
Poach fish in court-bouillon for 3-5 minutes until meat is flaky and white. Drain and allow fish to cool. Shred fish. Sauté onion and garlic in 1 tbsp. butter until soft. Add herbs, lemon juice, and fumet. Add shredded fish, then mix in chopped anchovy and ¼ cup breadcrumbs. In a mixer with a paddle attachment, combine fish mixture with 3 tbsp. softened butter and form into paste. Chill until cold and roll into balls. Coat with remaining breadcrumbs and fry in olive oil for 5-6 minutes or until lightly browned. Serve with Chorizo-Stuffed Creole Tomatoes and garnish with arugula.

CHORIZO-STUFFED CREOLE TOMATOES

4 Creole tomatoes
Salt and pepper to taste
2 tbsp. olive oil
½ lb. chorizo or other
   uncooked sausage
2 tbsp. diced celery

2 tbsp. diced onion
2 tsp. thyme
1 tbsp. finely chopped parsley
2 tbsp. breadcrumbs
2 tbsp. butter
¼ cup heavy cream

Méthode:
Halve tomatoes crosswise and hollow out the insides. Season lightly with salt and pepper and drizzle with olive oil. Arrange in a baking dish and roast in an oven at 375 degrees for 15-20 minutes until just tender. While tomatoes are roasting, remove chorizo from casing and chop finely. Cook in a heavy-bottomed pan over high heat for 2 minutes, until sausage releases some juice. Remove sausage from pan to colander, reserving 2 tbsp. fat in pan. Sweat celery and onion, covered, over low heat in reserved fat until translucent. Return chorizo to pan, then add thyme and parsley. In a sauté pan, toast breadcrumbs with butter until nutty in color; add to chorizo mixture. Allow mixture to cool then stir in cream. Stuff into roasted tomatoes and bake in 350-degree oven for 15-20 minutes or until heated through. Serve with Drum Croquettes.

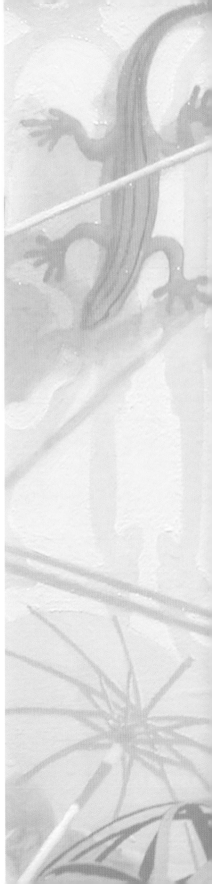

GROUPER *in a* PARMESAN BROTH *over* POLENTA
Serves 6

2 tbsp. olive oil
6 4-oz. grouper filets, skin on
Kosher salt to taste

Freshly ground black pepper to taste
2 tbsp. unsalted butter

Méthode:
Heat olive oil in sauté pan to the smoking point. Liberally season grouper on both sides with salt and pepper and place filets skin side down; cook over high heat until lightly browned. Add butter and turn fish. Lower heat to medium and cook fish through. Serve warm over Polenta and Parmesan Broth.

POLENTA

2 tbsp. olive oil
10 slices bacon, minced
¼ cup celery, minced
½ cup red onion, minced
2 tbsp. garlic, minced

2 cups milk
1 qt. water
2 cups polenta
1 tbsp. rosemary
Salt and pepper to taste

Méthode:
Render bacon in olive oil. Add celery, onion, and garlic and cook for 5-10 minutes. Add milk and water and bring to boil. Slowly whisk in polenta, stirring until it reaches a smooth and thick consistency. Finish with rosemary, salt, and pepper. Serve with Grouper.

PARMESAN BROTH

1 qt. fish stock
¼ cup fresh grated Parmesan

Méthode:
Heat stock in a pot over medium heat until hot but not boiling. Place grated Parmesan into cheese cloth and close securely. Add to broth and simmer for 12-15 minutes. Serve with Grouper and Polenta.

SCALLOPS *with* SMOKED TOMATO BUTTER
Serves 6

1 tbsp. black pepper
2 tsp. fennel seed
½ tsp. cayenne
1 tsp. paprika
2 tbsp. kosher salt

2 tbsp. olive oil
18 large sea scallops
½ lb. fresh Brussels sprouts,
    cut in half and blanched

Méthode:
Grind black pepper, fennel seed, cayenne, and paprika in a coffee mill to make a dry rub. Mix in kosher salt. Heat olive oil to the smoking point in a large nonstick pan. Season scallops with dry rub and sear in oil. Turn once and cook to medium; remove from pan and keep warm. Add Brussels sprouts and sear until brown. Serve Smoked Tomato Butter drizzled over Scallops and Brussels sprouts.

SMOKED TOMATO BUTTER

1 cup Smoked Tomato Coulis (recipe follows)
1 tsp. minced garlic
2 tsp. minced shallots
½ tsp. freshly ground black pepper
½ cup heavy cream
2 sticks butter
Salt to taste

Méthode:
Combine first 4 ingredients; reduce by half over medium to high heat. Add cream and reduce until thick. Whisk in butter and season with salt. Serve over Scallops.

SMOKED TOMATO COULIS

1 lb. smoked tomatoes
¼ cup crushed garlic
¼ cup sliced shallots
1 tbsp. black pepper
1 cup white wine
1 chipotle chili
1 tbsp. thyme

Méthode:
Simmer all ingredients for 30 minutes. Puree in blender and strain through a fine mesh sieve. Use as an ingredient in Smoked Tomato Butter.

coulis: heavy sauce usually made of one primary ingredient

SEAFOOD BOUCHÉE
Serves 2

1 tbsp. butter
3 oz. firm-fleshed whitefish
   such as drum, diced
6 Louisiana brown shrimp,
   peeled and deveined
¼ cup quartered mushrooms
1 tsp. chopped garlic
2 tsp. minced shallots

1 tsp. chopped parsley
Salt and pepper to taste
½ cup dry white wine
1 cup heavy cream
6 mussels, cleaned
2 puff pastry shells (or
   buttered toast points)

Méthode:
Heat butter in sauté pan until hot and foamy. Add fish, shrimp, and mushrooms; stirring, sauté 2 minutes. Stir in garlic, shallots, and parsley. Season with salt and pepper. Carefully add wine—it may flame!—and boil until volume is reduced by half. Add cream and mussels and simmer until thickened and the mussels have opened, about 5 minutes Correct the seasoning with salt and pepper. Spoon over puff pastry shells and serve hot.

Viandes & Volailles

CANARD à l'ORANGE
Serves 2-4

1 tsp. ground star anise seed
1 tsp. ground fennel seed
1 tsp. ground clove
1 tsp. ground black pepper

1 tsp. ground cinnamon
1 whole duck, rinsed and
  dried

Méthode:
Combine seasonings and rub over duck. Roast duck on rack in a 425-degree oven for 1½ hours or until the bird's internal temperature reaches 140 degrees. Remove from oven and allow to cool slightly. Quarter the duck and serve with Orange Sauce liberally applied.

ORANGE SAUCE

¼ cup finely chopped shallots
2 tbsp. orange zest
1 tbsp. butter
4 orange supremes
  (segments), diced meat only
½ cup orange liqueur

½ cup red wine
1 bay leaf
1 cup orange juice
2 cups veal glace
Salt and pepper to taste
2 sprigs thyme

Méthode:
Sweat shallots and zest in butter over low heat in a covered pan. Add supremes and cook until dry. Do not burn. Carefully deglaze with orange liqueur. Cook for 2-3 minutes over medium heat, then stir in red wine and bay leaf and reduce by half. Add orange juice; reduce by half. Add veal glace and simmer slowly, skimming to remove fat, until nappe. Season with salt, pepper, and thyme.

CANARD *with* CALVADOS SAUCE *and* ROSEMARY GNOCCHI

Serves 2-4

1 tsp. ground star anise seed
1 tsp. ground fennel seed
1 tsp. ground cloves
1 tsp. ground black pepper
1 tsp. ground cinnamon
1 whole duck, rinsed and dried
1 qt. apple juice

4 shallots, sliced
½ cup apple cider vinegar
2 whole star anise seeds
1 bay leaf
Bouquet of thyme sprigs
5 whole black peppercorns
2 qt. duck stock

Méthode:

Combine star anise, fennel, cloves, pepper, and cinnamon. Rub seasonings into the skin of the duck. Roast on a rack in a 425-degree oven for 1½ hours or until the bird's internal temperature reaches 140 degrees. Remove from oven and allow to cool slightly. Break down into quarters. Combine apple juice, shallots, vinegar, whole anise, bay leaf, thyme, and peppercorns in a large pot. Over high heat, bring to a boil and reduce by half. Add duck stock and reduce to nappe, a syrupy consistency. Strain reduction and serve over duck with Calvados Sauce and Rosemary Gnocchi.

CALVADOS SAUCE

2 cups apple juice
1 tbsp. chopped shallots
3 tbsp. red wine vinegar
1 star anise seed
1 bay leaf
Thyme sprigs

4 whole black peppercorns
1 cup duck or veal stock
1 cup veal stock
2 tbsp. apple jelly
2 tbsp. Calvados

Méthode:
Combine first 7 ingredients in a pot and bring to a boil; reduce by half. Add stock and reduce to nappe. Strain. Return to pot, add jelly and Calvados, and bring to boil. Reduce heat to a low simmer and reduce to a consistency of a light syrup. Serve over Duck.

ROSEMARY GNOCCHI

3 Yukon gold potatoes
2 egg yolks
1 tbsp. chopped rosemary
1 tsp. salt

1 tsp. pepper
½ cup flour
Oil

Méthode:
Roast potatoes until fully cooked, about 90 minutes. Discard peel and force potatoes through a mesh sieve. Add egg yolks, rosemary, salt, and pepper; mix lightly. Add flour until dough is soft and dry; it should not be sticky. Divide dough into quarters. Roll each piece into long, smooth snakes of dough as wide as a finger. Cut into 1-inch segments. Blanch in well-salted rapidly boiling water for 2 minutes. Shock in ice water and drain immediately. Add oil to moisten. Serve with Duck.

GAME HENS *WITH* CASSIS GASTRIQUE
Serves 2

4 Cornish hens, rinsed and
  dried
2 tbsp. butter, melted
1 tbsp. paprika
Salt and pepper to taste

½ bunch green onions,
  chopped
1 tbsp. butter
¼ cup chopped pecans
Wild rice, cooked

Méthode:
Coat hens with melted butter and season with paprika, salt, and
pepper. Roast on a wide rack in the oven at 350 degrees for 45
minutes or until juices run clear. In a sauté pan, wilt green onions
in butter; set aside. Arrange pecan pieces in a single layer on a
pan. Toast at 350 degrees for 10 minutes. Combine cooked rice,
pecans, and green onions. Serve hens over a bed of wild rice and
top with Cassis Gastrique.

CASSIS GASTRIQUE

½ cup sugar
¼ cup vinegar
½ cup crème de cassis

¼ cup demi-glace
½ cup lightly crushed red
  currants

Caramelize sugar in a medium-sized sauce pot over low heat.
Add vinegar to dissolve. Stir in cassis and demi-glace and
reduce by one-third. Add currants and reduce to nappe, a syrupy
consistency. Serve over Game Hens.

CHICKEN CASSIS
Serves 2-4

1 tbsp. kosher salt
1 tbsp. black pepper
6 fresh rosemary sprigs

1 (4 lb.) whole chicken, rinsed
   and dried
¼ cup extra-virgin olive oil

Méthode:
Combine the salt, pepper, and rosemary. Rub half the seasoning mixture inside the chicken cavity. Tie wings and legs against the back of the chicken. Place chicken breast side up on a rack above a roasting pan. Brush the chicken with olive oil. Rub the remaining seasoning mixture into the skin of the chicken. Roast the chicken in a 400-degree oven for 1½ hours, basting occasionally with juices until juices run clear and a leg bone easily pulls away from the meat. Remove from the oven and cover with tin foil. Allow to rest for 15 minutes before removing twine and quartering. Serve liberally with Cassis Sauce.

CASSIS SAUCE

¼ cup finely chopped shallots
Zest of 1 lemon
1 tbsp. butter
½ cup red currants
1 cup crème de cassis,
   divided

½ cup red wine
1 bay leaf
2 cups veal glace
Salt and pepper to taste
2 sprigs thyme

Méthode:
Sweat shallots and zest in butter over low heat in a covered pan. Add currants and cook until dry. Do not burn. Carefully deglaze with ½ cup crème de cassis. Cook for 2-3 minutes over medium heat, then stir in red wine and bay leaf and reduce by half. Add the remaining crème de cassis; reduce by half. Add veal glace and simmer slowly, skimming to remove fat, until nappe. Season with salt, pepper, and thyme.

CHICKEN BASQUAISE
Serves 6-8

4 oz. pancetta, julienned
3 tbsp. olive oil
1 whole chicken, cut into
    quarters, skin on
Salt and pepper to taste
½ cup sliced garlic
4 tsp. chili flakes
1 red onion, peeled and
    julienned
1 red pepper, stemmed,
    seeded, and julienned

1 green pepper, stemmed,
    seeded, and julienned
½ cup green olives (preferably
    unpitted Spanish)
2 tbsp. paprika
¼ cup chopped fresh parsley
1 tbsp. chopped fresh thyme
1 bay leaf
2 cups dry white wine
1 lb. cooked egg noodles

Méthode:

Crisp pancetta in olive oil until lightly rendered. Season chicken with salt and pepper, and brown skin side down in pan with pancetta. Add garlic and chili flakes and cook until garlic is browned. Add onion, lower heat, and cook slowly until onion is tender. Increase heat to medium, add peppers, olives, and paprika, and cook, stirring, until peppers are just tender, about 5 minutes. Add parsley, thyme, bay leaf, and wine. Simmer for 45 minutes and serve over egg noodles.

DIJON-CRUSTED RACK *of* LAMB *with* DEGAS HUSH PUPPIES

Serves 8

4 full lamb bone racks (4
   chops per person)
Salt and pepper to taste

2 tbsp. Dijon mustard
½ cup breadcrumbs

Méthode:
Sear the lamb chops on both sides. Remove from skillet and season with salt and pepper. Brush with olive oil and Dijon mustard, then dust with breadcrumbs. Cook in a 375-degree oven, basting frequently, until meat has cooked to desired temperature. Serve with Sauce and a side of Degas Hush Puppies.

SAUCE

2 tbsp. Dijon mustard
1 cup merlot
2 shallots, sliced
4 whole peppercorns
1 bay leaf

1 bouquet garni
1 qt. lamb stock (can be
   found at a specialty store or
   in powdered form)

Méthode:
Heat Dijon mustard, merlot, shallots, peppercorns, bay leaf, and bouquet garni over medium-high heat; reduce by half. Add lamb stock and simmer, skimming to remove fat, until reduced by one third. Strain Sauce through a fine mesh sieve. Pour over chops.

DEGAS HUSH PUPPIES
Yields 1 dozen

2 tbsp. minced onion
2 tbsp. diced green pepper
1 tsp. minced garlic
1 tbsp. butter
¼ cup flour
¼ cup cornmeal
¼ cup corn flour
1 tsp. baking powder
Pinch of salt
1 egg, beaten

¼ cup whole milk
1 tbsp. vegetable oil
Dash of Crystal hot sauce
Dash of Worcestershire sauce
Dash of granulated garlic
¼ tsp. cayenne
1 tsp. granulated sugar
Salt and pepper to taste
3 cups vegetable oil for frying

Méthode:
In a covered pan over low heat, sweat onion, pepper, and garlic in butter; cool. Combine flour, cornmeal, corn flour, baking powder, and salt then add cooked vegetables. Slowly mix beaten egg, milk, vegetable oil, hot sauce, and Worcestershire sauce into flour mixture; combine well, making sure there are no lumps. Add seasonings. Heat vegetable oil in a heavy-bottomed pan to 325 degrees. Dip an ice-cream scoop into a little oil to keep it from sticking and drop dough by scoopfuls into mixture. Fry until golden brown. Dry and serve with Dijon-Crusted Rack of Lamb.

BRAISED RABBIT *with* HARD APPLE CIDER
Serves 2-4

1 rabbit, quartered
Salt and pepper to taste
½ cup all-purpose flour
¼ cup extra-virgin olive oil
2 large onions, chopped

6 garlic cloves, minced
1 lb. Crimini mushrooms
1 qt. demi-glace
1 12 oz. bottle hard cider

Méthode:
Season rabbit with salt and pepper. Dredge in flour. Place in 4 qt. brazier pot or rondeau with olive oil heated to the smoking point. Brown rabbit deeply. Remove from pot and set aside. Add olive oil to pot and sauté onions and garlic until they caramelize. Add mushrooms and cook lightly for about 3 minutes. Return rabbit to pot; add demi-glace and cider. Place pot in a 350-degree oven covered for 1½ hours or until rabbit is tender.

PORK CHOP FOYOT *with* ORANGE BUTTER SAUCE
Serves 2

2 ¼-inch cut pork chop
5 tbsp. extra-virgin olive oil
Salt and pepper to taste
1 large onion, chopped

⅓ cup butter
¾ cup Gruyère, grated
½ cup breadcrumbs

Méthode:
Marinate chop in olive oil for 1 hour. Remove from marinade and season with salt and pepper. Brown chop in a sauté pan for 3 minutes on each side. Place in a 350-degree oven for an additional 3-4 minutes. Set aside. In a pot, caramelize onion lightly in ⅓ cup butter. Do not brown. Top pork chop with onion, cheese, and breadcrumbs. Broil until the cheese is melted and lightly browned. Serve with Orange Butter Sauce.

ORANGE BUTTER SAUCE

2 large shallots, chopped
½ cup white wine
½ cup vinegar

⅓ cup butter
½ cup heavy cream
6 tbsp. orange concentrate

Méthode:
Wilt shallots in the butter used to caramelize the onion for the Pork Chop Foyot. Add the white wine and vinegar and reduce over medium heat until the liquid is gone. Add cream and remove from heat. Slowly add the remaining ⅓ cup butter until it is incorporated into the mixture. Season to taste. Gently stir in the orange concentrate. Serve liberally over Pork Chop Foyot.

FILET *with* ST. JOHN BUTTER
Serves 6

6 5-oz. filets
Kosher salt and cracked black
   pepper to taste

Méthode:
After preparing the St. John Butter and Filet Sauce, season filets liberally with kosher salt and cracked black pepper. Sear in a hot pan or on a grill to desired temperature. Place a disk of St. John Butter on top and serve with Filet Sauce.

ST. JOHN BUTTER

¼ cup red wine
1 tbsp. chopped garlic
2 tsp. chopped shallots
1 stick butter
2 oz. blue cheese, crumbled

4 tbsp. chopped parsley
Dash of Tabasco or Crystal
   hot sauce
Juice from ½ lemon

Méthode:
In a small sauté pan, boil red wine with garlic and shallots until almost dry. Combine wine mixture and all remaining ingredients in a food processor and mix until smooth. Refrigerate. Once it has chilled, form butter mixture into cylinders by scooping out the semi-hardened butter and shaping it into a thick line on cellophane sheets. Wrap the cellophane around the butter and roll it into long cylinders about the diameter of a half dollar. Chill in ice water or refrigerate. Slice into small pads of butter and allow to melt over Filet.

FILET SAUCE

1 cup finely chopped onion
1 small carrot, finely chopped
1 rib finely chopped celery
2 tbsp. vegetable oil
1 tbsp. butter
½ cup brandy
2 tbsp. finely chopped fresh
  thyme

1 tbsp. finely chopped fresh
  rosemary
1 bay leaf
4 whole black peppercorns
4 whole green peppercorns
Filet cuttings
1 qt. blond veal stock

Méthode:

In a large pot, sauté the onion, carrot, and celery in oil and butter until caramelized. Deglaze the pan with brandy and add thyme, rosemary, bay leaf, and peppercorns. Add any cuttings, fatty trim, or juices from filet to the mixture. Add veal stock and bring to a boil; reduce by half. Strain, shock in a cold water bath, and skim off all the fat. Serve with Filet.

DEGAS GRILLADES *and* GRITS
Serves 4-5

1 lb. veal stew or shoulder
   meat, rinsed and dried
1½ tsp. kosher salt
1 tsp. black pepper
1 tsp. paprika
1 tbsp. olive oil
½ cup diced onion
¼ cup diced celery
1½ tsp. minced garlic
2 tbsp. diced green pepper
2 tbsp. diced red pepper
2 tbsp. flour
½ cup white wine

1 cup diced tomatoes
½ cup beef stock
1 bay leaf
½ tsp. fresh thyme
1½ tsp. Worcestershire sauce
½ tsp. Tabasco or Crystal hot
   sauce
Pinch of cayenne
Fresh grated Parmesan
   cheese for garnish
Sliced green onions for
   garnish

Méthode:

Season veal with salt, black pepper, and paprika. Brown in olive oil and drain in a colander; set aside. In a large rondeau, sauté mirepoix (onion, celery, garlic, and peppers) until tender. Stir in flour and cook until flour is fully blended. Add wine and reduce by half. Puree tomatoes in a blender and add to rondeau. Mix in beef stock and simmer for 30 minutes. Add cooked veal, bay leaf, thyme, Worcestershire sauce, hot sauce, and cayenne; cover with aluminum foil and braise in a 350-degree oven until tender, about 1½ hours. Serve over grits and garnish with Parmesan and green onions.

HANGER STEAK *with* FRITES
serves 4-6

2 tbsp. vegetable oil
2 lb. hanger steak

Kosher salt and black pepper
    to taste

Note:
The hanger steak is also known as the butcher's cut.

Méthode:
Heat vegetable oil to the smoking point in a heavy-bottomed sauté pan. Season cleaned hanger steak with kosher salt and pepper; sear and cook to desired temperature. Let steak rest for 3-4 minutes to capture juices, then slice against the grain. Serve with Pommes Frites and Steak Sauce.

STEAK SAUCE

1 cup sliced shallots
1 cup sliced garlic
1 tbsp. butter
1 cup red wine
1 bay leaf

1 bouquet garni
1 qt. veal stock
Salt and pepper to taste
1 tbsp. chopped fresh parsley

Méthode:

Over high heat, caramelize shallots and garlic in butter. Add red wine, bay leaf, and bouquet garni; reduce by half. Lower heat then add veal stock and simmer, skimming to remove fat, until reduced by half. Season with salt, pepper, and parsley. Serve over Hanger Steak.

POMMES FRITES

3 large Idaho potatoes
3 cups vegetable oil
Kosher salt to taste

Méthode:

Peel and cut potatoes into bâtonnets. Rinse and soak in cold water, drain, and dry very well. Heat oil to 325 degrees and quick-fry potatoes for about 1 minute. Allow potatoes to cool. Raise fryer temperature to 375 degrees and fry again until golden brown. Drain well and season with kosher salt. Serve with Hanger Steak.

bâtonnet: foods cut into matchstick shapes; julienned

PANÉED VEAL *with* LEMON CAPER BUTTER
Serves 6

6 4-oz. veal flank cutlets
Salt and pepper to taste
1 cup all-purpose flour
2 eggs, beaten
½ cup breadcrumbs
1 tbsp. parsley
1 tbsp. Parmesan

1 tbsp. herbes de Provence
2 cups olive oil
½ cup butter
Capers for garnish
Fresh grated Parmesan for
   garnish

Méthode:

Pound veal to at least a quarter-inch thickness. Season with salt and pepper. Dredge in flour and set aside. Beat eggs into flour and then stir in breadcrumbs, parsley, Parmesan, and herbes de Provence. Dredge veal through flour mixture again. Pan-fry breaded veal in olive oil; flip over and add butter to pan. Veal should achieve a golden brown hue. Serve with generous amounts of Lemon Caper Butter and garnish with capers and Parmesan.

LEMON CAPER BUTTER

Juice of 3 lemons
Zest of 3 lemons
1 shallot, minced
3 star anise seeds
½ cup white wine
¼ cup rice wine vinegar

1 tbsp. capers, divided
1 tbsp. heavy cream
2 tbsp. butter
1½ tsp. salt
2 tbsp. unsalted butter

Méthode:

Combine first 6 ingredients and half of the capers; reduce over medium heat until almost dry. Do not burn. Add cream and reduce to thicken slightly. Whisk in both the salted and unsalted butter. Heat until nearly boiling and add salt. Serve over Panéed Veal.

Desserts

bain-marie: a hot water bath used to cook foods gently or to keep cooked foods hot; consists of placing a container of food in a large, shallow pan of warm water

ÎLES FLOTTANTES (FLOATING ISLANDS)
Serves 10-12

16 eggs, separated; reserve yolks for Crème Anglaise

½ tbsp. salt
½ lb. sugar

Méthode:
Whisk egg whites with salt to form a solid foam. Whisk in sugar. Divide among individual 4 oz. aluminum cups. Place in the oven in a bain-marie, or water bath, for 20 minutes at 350 degrees. Remove, allow to cool, and then refrigerate. To serve, remove from aluminum cups and place in individual bowls with ladled Crème Anglaise. Serve cold.

CRÈME ANGLAISE

1½ cups heavy cream
2 vanilla beans

6 egg yolks
½ cup sugar

Méthode:
Heat cream and vanilla over medium heat. Whisk yolks and sugar in a separate bowl until the mixture turns white. Add yolk and sugar mixture to the pot with the cream. Cook over low heat for 3 minutes, whisking continuously. Remove from heat. Allow to cool and then refrigerate. Ladle over Îles Flottantes.

CARAMEL BREAD PUDDING
Serves 12-16

2 baguettes, diced
1 stick butter, melted
1½ cups sugar
5 eggs
1 tbsp. vanilla extract

4 cups milk
4 cups brandy milk punch
1 tbsp. cinnamon
1 tsp. nutmeg

Méthode:
Toss diced baguettes with melted butter in a large oven-safe pan. Toast in the oven at 350 degrees until golden brown. Beat sugar and eggs together in a bowl until smooth. Add all remaining ingredients to sugar-egg mixture; combine. Add toasted bread to liquid mixture and soak until bread is well saturated. Pour into a roasting pan and bake in a water bath at 350 degrees for about 90 minutes. Serve covered in Caramel Sauce.

CARAMEL SAUCE

2 cups sugar
¼ cup water
4 cups cream

Méthode:
Stirring constantly, cook sugar in a heavy-bottomed saucepan over medium heat. As sugar melts, remove from heat while continuing to stir. Fold in water using extreme caution. Return to burner and bring to a boil. Boil until sugar turns golden brown. Add cream then return to a boil. Remove from heat and cool. Serve over Caramel Bread Pudding.

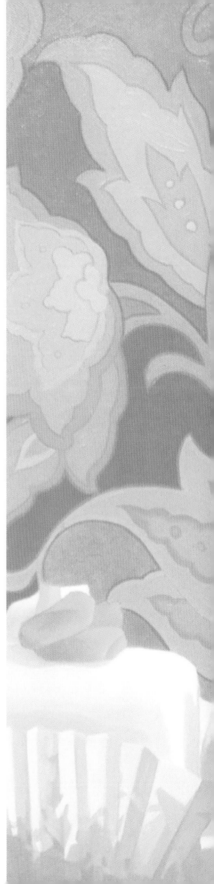

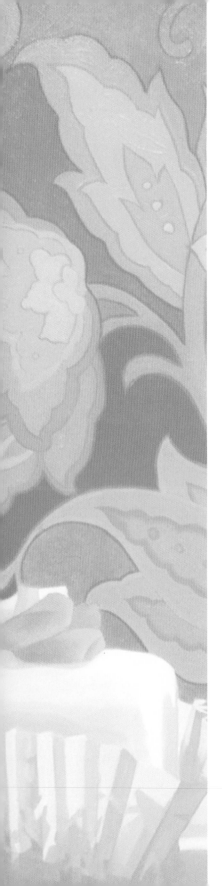

CRÈME BRÛLÉE
Serves 12

15 egg yolks
1½ cups sugar

4½ cups heavy cream
2 tbsp. vanilla extract

Méthode:
In a large bowl, whip egg yolks and sugar together until light and ribbons form. In a pot, bring cream and vanilla to a boil. Whisk boiling cream and vanilla into egg yolks. Pour into ramekins and bake for 45-60 minutes at 325 degrees in a bain-marie, or water bath, until the mixture becomes firm. Dust sugar onto the tops of the crème in the ramekins. Using a torch, caramelize the sugar on top until it reaches a beautiful light golden brown color. (A broiler may be used instead of a torch.) Allow to cool slightly before serving.

DARK CHOCOLATE MOUSSE
Serves 6-8

4 oz. chocolate chips
¾ cup butter
1 cup heavy cream, warmed
2 egg yolks

4 egg whites
2 tbsp. sugar
1 unflavored gelatin pack
2 tsp. orange liqueur

Méthode:
Melt chocolate and butter together in a double boiler. Temper or mix in warm cream and fold in egg yolks. In a bowl, whip egg whites with sugar until stiff. Warm whites then mix into chocolate. Fold in tempered gelatin and orange liqueur. Chill and serve.

LAVENDER HONEY CRÈME CARAMEL
Serves 12

1¾ cups sugar, divided
Dash of lemon juice
6 tbsp. water
15 egg yolks

½ cup honey
4½ cups heavy cream
1 tbsp. vanilla
¼ tsp. lavender oil

Méthode:
Butter ramekins. Combine 1 cup sugar and lemon juice for caramel in a heavy-bottomed saucepan. Stirring constantly, cook over medium heat. As sugar melts, remove from heat while continuing to stir. Fold in water using extreme caution. Return to burner and bring to a boil. Boil until sugar turns golden brown. Divide among ramekins. In a bowl, whip together egg yolks, honey, and ¾ cup sugar until light and ribbons form; set aside. Bring cream to a boil. Whisk boiling cream, vanilla, and lavender oil into egg yolks. Pour into ramekins and bake at 325 degrees in a bain-marie, or water bath, for approximately 1 hour and 45 minutes or until done.

Desserts

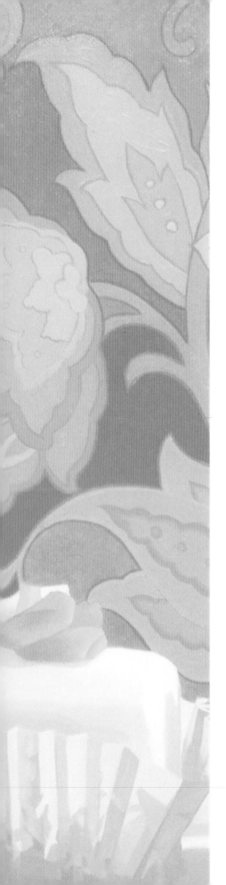

LEMON ICEBOX PIE
Yields 1 10" pie

3 sticks butter, melted
1 lb. graham cracker meal
6 egg yolks
1¼ cups bottled lemon juice

Juice of 2½ lemons
Zest of 2½ lemons
Zest of 1 lime
3 cups condensed milk

Méthode:
In a mixer with a paddle attachment, slowly mix melted butter into graham cracker meal. Press evenly into a 10" greased and floured pie tin. Bake at 350 degrees for 15 minutes or until golden brown. While crust is baking, whisk together yolks, juice, zest, and condensed milk. Pour filling into baked pie shell. Freeze overnight. Serve frozen topped with whipped cream.

PEANUT BUTTER PIE
Yields 1 9" pie

1 cup graham cracker crumbs
¼ cup sugar
¼ cup butter, softened
1 8-oz. package cream
  cheese, softened
1 cup creamy peanut butter

1 cup + 2 tbsp. confectioners'
  sugar, divided
1 cup heavy cream, divided
1 tbsp. vanilla extract
1 cup semisweet chocolate
  morsels

Méthode:

In a bowl combine cracker crumbs, sugar, and butter; mix thoroughly. Press into a buttered 9-inch pie pan, forming a shell. Refrigerate 1 hour. In a large bowl beat together the softened cream cheese, 2 tbsp. softened butter, and peanut butter with an electric mixer. Add 1 cup confectioners' sugar and beat until fluffy. In a separate bowl beat ½ cup cream until a peak forms. Gradually add 2 tbsp. confectioners' sugar and vanilla and beat to a stiff peak. Fold the beaten cream into the peanut butter mixture, mixing well. Transfer the filling to the shell and refrigerate until firm, 2-3 hours. While pie is chilling bring ½ cup heavy cream to a simmer over low heat. Add chocolate and stir until melted and smooth. Cool to room temperature. After the filling has firmed, spread the topping over the pie. Return to refrigerator until the topping is firm, about 3 hours. Cut into 8 pieces and serve.

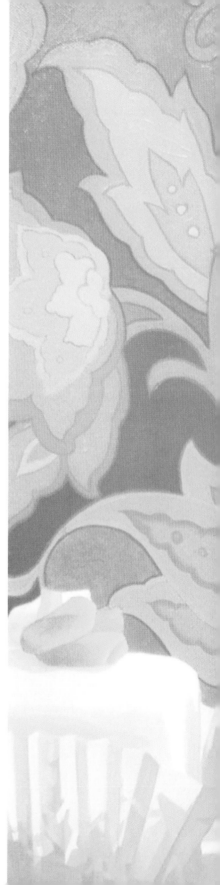

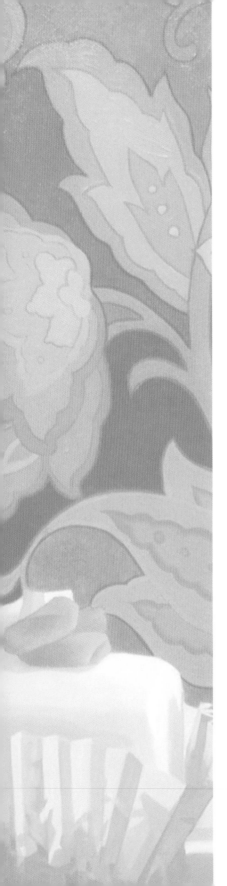

TARTE TATIN
Yields 1 10" tart

4 tbsp. butter	¼ tsp. cinnamon
1 cup brown sugar	½ tsp. vanilla
3 cups apple slices	1 rolled pâte sucrée or other
2 tsp. lemon juice	pastry dough

Méthode:
Preheat oven to 450 degrees. Melt butter in a 9" baking dish. Add brown sugar and, stirring, heat over medium-high heat for 3 minutes, until the bubbles are large and heavy. Cool slightly until sugar begins to set. Cover with sliced apples in an attractive pattern. Blend lemon juice, cinnamon, and vanilla; sprinkle over apple slices. Cover with pastry dough. Trim to fit but do not seal edges. Bake for 15-20 minutes until pastry is golden brown. Cool for 2 minutes and invert onto serving platter. Serve with whipped cream or crème fraîche.

WHITE CHOCOLATE *and* PECAN BUTTER
Yields 1 cup

¼ cup white chocolate
1 stick butter, melted
10 pecans, chopped
Salt to taste

Brandy to taste
¾ cup white corn syrup (or
    other inert sugar)

Méthode:
Fold chocolate into melted butter. Gently heat to melt chocolate, removing from heat if necessary to prevent burning. Add pecans. Season with salt and brandy, then mix in corn syrup. Chill. Serve drizzled over ice cream.

RED-WINE-POACHED PEARS *over* VANILLA ICE CREAM
Serves 5

¼ cup orange juice
½ qt. red wine
½ qt. water
½ cup sugar
1 cinnamon stick, ground
3 cloves, ground

1 tbsp. allspice, ground
3 bay leaves
2 tbsp. orange zest
1 tsp. nutmeg
5 pears, peeled and seeded

Méthode:
Combine all ingredients except pears. Bring to a boil and simmer for 1 hour. Add pears to mixture and poach until very soft. Serve with Vanilla Ice Cream.

VANILLA ICE CREAM
Yields 1 gallon

3 14-oz. cans sweetened
    condensed milk
6 cups milk
6 tbsp. heavy cream

15 egg yolks, beaten
1½ tsp. vanilla extract
1½ tsp. salt

Méthode:
Simmer condensed milk, milk, and heavy cream, then fold egg yolks into mixture. Cook for 2-3 minutes or until thickened. Fold in vanilla and salt. Place in ice cream maker and follow the directions for the machine. Serve topped with Red-Wine-Poached Pears.

Note:
The ice cream mixture can be flavored with a multitude of liqueurs, either added directly to the mix or poured directly over the vanilla base. Creativity should reign here. Think cassis, Framboise, or peaches, for example.

MEASUREMENT
CONVERSION CHART

ABBREVIATIONS

STANDARD			METRIC		
tsp.	=	teaspoon	ml.	=	milliliter
tbsp.	=	tablespoon	l.	=	liter
oz.	=	ounce	g.	=	gram
qt.	=	quart	kg.	=	kilogram
lb.	=	pound	mg.	=	milligram

STANDARD-METRIC APPROXIMATIONS

⅛ teaspoon = .6 milliliter
¼ teaspoon = 1.2 milliliters
½ teaspoon = 2.5 milliliters
1 teaspoon = 5 milliliters
1 tablespoon = 15 milliliters
4 tablespoons = ¼ cup = 60 milliliters
8 tablespoons = ½ cup = 118 milliliters
16 tablespoons = 1 cup = 236 milliliters
2 cups = 473 milliliters
2½ cups = 563 milliliters
4 cups = 946 milliliters
1 quart = 4 cups = .94 liter

SOLID MEASUREMENTS

½ ounce = 15 grams
1 ounce = 25 grams
4 ounces = 110 grams
16 ounces = 1 pound = 454 grams

INDEX